D0250370

"Here's a guide from the heart of Bernie's grassroots movement that mobilized hundreds of thousands of volunteers. *Rules for Revolutionaries* is a playbook for 'big organizing'—a melding of grassroots movement tactics with new technology. It's a must-read for anyone who wants to take back our economy from the moneyed interests."

—Robert B. Reich, author of *Saving Capitalism*

"*Rules for Revolutionaries* is a lamppost for those who are committed to causes of community uplift, grassroots empowerment, and organizing for good. Insurgents get ready, this is the book for you." **—Nina Turner**, assistant professor of African American history, Cuyahoga Community College; national surrogate, Bernie Sanders campaign; former Ohio state senator

"This must-read book lays down twenty-two 'rules' designed to put power in the hands of people who want to make radical social change. Becky Bond and Zack Exley have walked the walk—and they know what organizing looks like when you begin with a big, transformative demand and challenge the establishment. You win big when you ask big—and whoever wins in November, we'll need to push for revolutionary change from Day One. Becky and Zack's book is a vital contribution to that project!" **—Katrina vanden Heuvel**, editor and publisher, *The Nation*

"Crucial, important, strategic, urgent."

—Naomi Wolf, *New York Times* bestselling author of *The End of America*

NO LONGER PROPERTY OF RECEIVED
SEATTLE PUBLIC LIBRARY
APR 2017

LAKE CITY LIBRARY

Praise for
Rules for Revolutionaries

"Two of our generation's most accomplished organizers share the creative tactics and technology they used to lead hundreds of thousands of people to volunteer their time to change the course of history—and how you can, too. This page-turner belongs in the hands of new and veteran organizers alike and will set the standard for how to make change in the twenty-first century."

—David Broockman, assistant professor of political economy, Stanford University

"Becky and Zack's rules are as refreshing as Bernie's candidacy itself. Their rules are specific enough to get started right now and flexible enough to last for the long haul of the revolution we so desperately need."

—Tim DeChristopher, Bidder 70; cofounder, Climate Disobedience Center

"If you want to change the world and the status quo, read this book. An alternate title would appropriately be: *How to Make the Impossible, Possible.* Prepare to be inspired."

—Assemblywoman Lucy Flores

"For populists who want to continue Bernie Sanders's political revolution and win radical change, this is a book for you. In their *Rules for Revolutionaries*, Becky Bond and Zack Exley lay down a new marker for what mass volunteer organizing makes possible by combining emerging consumer technology and radical trust with some tried and true 'old organizing' tactics."

—Jim Hightower, author of *Swim Against the Current*

"Bernie Sanders's presidential run was a spectacular wake-up call, revealing the huge number of Americans willing to fight for radical change. That includes a great many who didn't sign up for the political revolution this time around, which is good news: Our movements can learn how to go even bigger and broader. We can win—but only if we continue to develop the kinds of tactics, tools, and vision laid out in this vitally important book, perhaps the first to explore how to organize at the true scale of the crises we face."

—Naomi Klein,
author of *This Changes Everything*
and *The Shock Doctrine*

"Climate activists around the world watched Bernie's vibrant volunteer network with envy and wondered whether we, too, could build that level of engagement absent a candidate and national election. Bond and Exley answer that question: Yes, we can! Everyone who wants to solve climate change—or any other big issue—should read this book and get started."

—Annie Leonard, Greenpeace USA

"If you want to understand Bernie's remarkable campaign— and more importantly, if you want to understand how to organize big, world-shaking campaigns of all kinds in the future—this is the book for you. The authors bring enormous credibility and enormous insight to a crucial task; what they describe in electoral politics goes just as much for battles like the one around the Keystone pipeline."

—Bill McKibben,
New York Times bestselling author;
cofounder, 350.org

RULES
— FOR —
REVOLUTIONARIES

RULES
— FOR —
REVOLUTIONARIES

★ ★ ★ ★ HOW ★ ★ ★ ★
BIG ORGANIZING
CAN CHANGE
EVERYTHING

BECKY BOND AND ZACK EXLEY

Chelsea Green Publishing
White River Junction, Vermont

Copyright © 2016 by Becky Bond and Zack Exley.
All rights reserved.

No part of this book may be transmitted or
reproduced in any form by any means without
permission in writing from the publisher.

Project Manager: Patricia Stone
Project Editor: Brianne Goodspeed
Copy Editor: Deborah Heimann
Proofreader: Angela Boyle
Designer: Melissa Jacobson

Printed in the United States of America.

First printing November, 2016.
10 9 8 7 6 5 4 3 2 1   16 17 18 19 20

Our Commitment to Green Publishing
Chelsea Green sees publishing as a tool for cultural change and ecological stewardship.
We strive to align our book manufacturing practices with our editorial mission and to
reduce the impact of our business enterprise in the environment. We print our books
and catalogs on chlorine-free recycled paper, using vegetable-based inks whenever possible. This book may cost slightly more because it was printed on paper that contains
recycled fiber, and we hope you'll agree that it's worth it. Chelsea Green is a member of
the Green Press Initiative (www.greenpressinitiative.org), a nonprofit coalition of publishers, manufacturers, and authors working to protect the world's endangered forests
and conserve natural resources. The text pages of *Rules for Revolutionaries* were printed
on paper supplied by QuadGraphics that contains 100% postconsumer recycled fiber.

ISBN 978-1-60358-727-3 (paperback)—ISBN 978-1-60358-728-0 (ebook)

Library of Congress Cataloging-in-Publication Data is available upon request.

Chelsea Green Publishing
85 North Main Street, Suite 120
White River Junction, VT 05001
(802) 295-6300
www.chelseagreen.com

For the volunteers
who are leading the political revolution

Contents

Preface

★ becky ★

"This is how we win." That was the subject line of the first email I wrote back in the fall of 2015 to the rapidly growing list of Bernie Sanders supporters. It was 6:00 a.m., and Zack and I were occupying the lobby of a Comfort Inn in Little Rock, Arkansas.

While brilliant field veterans Robert Becker and Julia Barnes were building incredible traditional campaigns on the ground in Iowa and New Hampshire, Zack and I found ourselves on a team of go-for-broke irregulars charged with organizing what was then a vast outpost of the Bernie Sanders campaign for president. It was our task to help organize supporters in all the states that would not be staffed until much later in the primary campaign cycle.

Of course, Bernie didn't win the primary, and that was heartbreaking for so many of us. As Zack and I finish up the writing of this book, we are watching the polls tighten in the race between Donald Trump and Hillary Clinton. A race that all polls have indicated would have been a cakewalk for Bernie. Meanwhile, the police continue to murder unarmed black people seemingly with impunity, and Native American tribes are leading an epic human rights protest blocking the route of a new oil pipeline from breaking sacred ground in North Dakota. We don't know yet who will win the 2016 general election or the outcome of social justice confrontations that are reaching a boiling point. But we do know that no matter what happens next there is a new and better way forward for those of us fighting for social change.

In his inspiring run for the presidency, Bernie broke a lot of rules and challenged the conventional wisdom. Along the way, the volunteer grassroots movement that helped propel his campaign learned a whole new set of rules. Rules that can help grow the political revolution Bernie called for and revolutionize the work of social movements in the United States and around the world.

Before I left my job to work on the Bernie Sanders campaign, I was privileged to work for fifteen years at what was first known as Working Assets and then became CREDO. There I helped create and scale CREDO Action, and cofounded CREDO SuperPAC.

At CREDO I learned from my boss Michael Kieschnick to think big, to manage people and campaigns with tough love, and to look to science and testing to ensure resources were best deployed in the often asymmetrical battles waged from the progressive flank. It was through Michael that I was first introduced to the quantitative political scientist Donald Green. Green was among the first academics to apply randomized control trial methodology to the study of American voting behavior. His field experiments and field experiments inspired by his work have led to a hugely influential and growing body of science-based evidence detailing which voter turnout tactics have the greatest impact at the lowest cost.

Research shows that, contrary to the conventional wisdom, the big money approach to elections isn't what really moves voters. When it comes to moving voters to the polls in elections, it's not the broadcast television ads that matter. Campaign robocalls make a difference only to the consultant who earns money making them. Direct mail doesn't have much of an effect. As it turns out, when you look at the actual campaign results, the gold standard for moving voters in elections is a volunteer having a conversation with a voter on the doorstep or on the telephone.

This is great news for everyone who believes our country needs radical change. It will be hard to dispel the myth that spending big money on advertising is the path to electoral victory, but we do know that if people organize, we can go up against big money and win.

But there is so much money in politics these days—seemingly limitless amounts. Is it really possible to scale grassroots participation to a height that could actually let us go toe to toe with the billionaires and win?

That's the question that Zack and I both left our day jobs and joined the Bernie Sanders campaign to answer. Our experiment in grassroots participation was situated on the fringes of the Bernie campaign. We were part of a small department dedicated to distributed organizing that worked outside of the traditional campaign field operation that comprised paid staffers running field offices in key states. It was our job to scale grassroots involvement in a strategic campaign at the national level.

By the end of the campaign, as part of our program more than one hundred thousand volunteers had made calls to voters, with tens of thousands of regular callers who made practically a part-time job out of it. They made more than seventy-five million calls. A few thousand volunteers individually sent over eight million text messages. More than one hundred thousand volunteer-led events were held, and more than one thousand "barnstorm" mass meetings were led, which fed much of this activity. It was amazing. Not only were the numbers of people getting involved big, but the time and resources people were willing to put into their fight for Bernie were astounding.

We want to be clear we were responsible for only one piece of the campaign. Zack and I spent most of the campaign in volunteer outposts that were generally beyond the reach of the traditional field operation, working with volunteers to forge a new set of rules to embrace and scale a growing movement of people willing to do something big to win something big. From the point of view of many of the traditional staffers on the campaign, we were the fringe—an almost totally irrelevant part of the campaign.

For many of the hundreds of thousands of volunteers we interacted with through our various platforms, our small team, which came to be known as the "distributed organizing team," was their main connection to the campaign, and we were the people who were supposed to help them put Bernie over the top. We had an urgent mandate, access to mostly consumer software, and a huge number of volunteers ready to do whatever it would take to make Bernie the Democratic nominee. All that combined gave us the opportunity to overthrow some of the current orthodoxies, to write new rules, and to reach back in organizing history to bring back some old ones.

This book is not an inside account of the Bernie campaign, and it's not a book about elections. It's a book about organizing. We're writing this book to share the new rules that emerged from our work on the Bernie campaign and in our long careers at the intersection of technology and social change organizing. It felt like we were just getting started when the primary came to an end. But we learned enough along the way to know that if the people who read this book put some of these rules into practice, and maybe write some rules of their own, we can win solutions that are as radical as the problems we face.

Preface

★ zack ★

This book has gone to the printer before the 2016 presidential election, so we don't know whether Clinton or Trump is the president as you're reading this. America either just narrowly survived its first brush with actual fascism, or we just learned that, yes, it *can* happen here. Either way, we believe that the rules in this book provide some of the answers for the struggle ahead.

No matter who wins in 2016, the revolution is here. In democracies, people do not accept decline forever. Real wages have been falling for forty years. Our maternal mortality rate has fallen behind every developed nation in the world and many developing nations. Forty percent of Americans will live below the poverty line at some point in their lives. Tens of millions of children who grew up in middle class homes are finding themselves firmly in the working class. Criminal justice systems at every level of government prey upon Americans of all backgrounds but disproportionately on African Americans and Latinos.

As should have been expected, when candidates emerged who were talking about the decline—and offering to do something about it—millions of voters backed them, despite how unconventional they were and despite all the baggage they carried. Bernie almost won the Democratic nomination, and Trump—defying anyone's sense of what was possible—did win. As things get worse and worse, voters will support candidates who promise radical action. And if there are no principled alternatives emerging on the left, this creates an opening for right-wing candidates like Trump, no matter how reprehensible and no matter how crazy their solutions may be. This is a well-established pattern in history for democracies in crisis.

If you believe America should be a multiracial, multiethnic society, if you believe in welcoming immigrants, if you believe in peace, and if you believe that we as a people should be able to deliberately improve our economic situation—then you need to get involved in the project of presenting the American people with solutions to the problems that are tearing Americans' lives to shreds. If you don't, then the fascists are going to win.

Trump let the genie out of the bottle. For three presidential cycles, Democrats brought in hundreds of millions of small donations while Republicans never figured it out. Trump figured it out—and called his run "not a campaign but a movement." As long as Americans' standards of living and freedoms are in decline, more and more competent fascists are going to come along to hijack our democracy until one finally wins.

We must put a practical and radical path forward that the American people feel welcome to try! If you're an activist, campaign volunteer, or professional political operative who is in this for the right reasons, then pointing that way forward and making it possible will be the work of the rest of your life.

The way forward isn't simply a matter of winning elections— though electing revolutionaries to office at all levels of government is some of the necessary work of the revolution. We need deep healing and transformation in every sphere of our society. Passing laws and paying for government programs will not even scratch the surface of what must be done. This will require organic mass movements in neighborhoods, towns, cities, and regions. It will require unions and small business associations organizing not simply to demand concessions from big businesses but to actively reshape the economy. It will require students, parents, teachers, administrators, and community members organizing and participating effectively to make our schools places where children get world-class educations. It will require creating revolutionary change through every sphere of our society.

I've been dreaming of working with Becky since we met way back in 2000. But the idea of writing a book about organizing with her was something I never could have imagined! The Bernie campaign helped realize some other dreams, too. Having worked on the internet's cutting edge in other insurgent presidential campaigns, in some big roles and some small roles, I knew that presidential campaigns were laboratories where magic happened and new ways of organizing were invented. Becky and I have both long seen the potential to reignite mass movement organizing, and we have been trying to help do that throughout our careers wherever we were.

When Bernie called for a political revolution, thousands of local volunteer leaders leapt to their feet and started organizing. Because of the beautiful quirks of Bernie's campaign, Claire Sandberg, Becky, and I were given the green light—or more accurately, a flashing yellow light—to multiply those volunteers and make them effective in the voter contact work that wins primaries and caucuses. We were given this role over states that the campaign for a long time didn't care about—and that became critical to winning in the later stages of the primary season.

The tools and methods that our distributed organizing team practiced in collaboration with Bernie volunteers across forty-six states are not brilliant new inventions. They are just a part of good old-fashioned mass movement organizing coming back to life—shaped by the communications technologies of the day—in an environment that made it easy for people like us to orchestrate their resurrection.

We believe these tools and methods are applicable to all kinds of organizing at any level.

We tried to keep this book focused on the Bernie campaign and tried to keep it short. But I would have loved to tell some stories about using some of these rules in small union campaigns with low-wage and immigrant workers, in student antiracism organizing, and in antiwar organizing. What a presidential campaign allows is the opportunity to show how this stuff can function at scale. That is thanks to several factors: the number of people involved, the volunteer software developers who come out of the woodwork to build new tools, the availability of straightforward work (voter contact work) that everyone can do, and the uncomplicated and undebatable goal of the campaign to elect a new president.

But now that these tools and methods for bringing mass movement organizing have been demonstrated, opportunities for all organizations and all movements are manifest. Just as earlier presidential campaigns opened up a whole new world for online fundraising, we hope that Bernie's campaign can do the same for mass movement organizing.

As this book goes to press, we are living in a moment when mass protest is in the news frequently and making a big impact on our politics. The whole world has been having a bit of an epiphany over the past few decades around the topic of mass protest—from the "Color Revolutions" to the Arab Spring and from the antiglobalization movement to Occupy Wall Street to the movement to defend black lives. We wholeheartedly endorse what's been developing.

AND we want to see leaders from movements like these actually take power. A protest movement is not successful if it knocks out an establishment only to replace it with a newer, fresher one that holds the same values and agenda as the old one. Some people in the our movements believe strongly that we should not take power—that we should simply build stronger and stronger protest movements that will eventually wipe away the very existence of power. We respect that view but don't share it. We want to see the people take power. And we believe that right now, the people are closer than ever to making that happen.

We humbly submit these rules for revolutionaries in hope that they will help.

Why Big Organizing

★ becky & zack ★

In this book we're going to talk about big organizing. It's a way to understand mass revolutionary organizing that's relevant today. Mass revolutionary organizing is what powered virtually every transformational movement in US history from anticolonial rebellions up through the civil rights, women's rights, and gay rights movements.

By the end of the twentieth century, however, big organizing had been almost completely supplanted by a plodding, one-by-one organizing orthodoxy that we call small organizing. The rise of small organizing is a complex story involving the professionalization of politics, attempts by the liberal establishment to channel radical impulses of working class people and people of color into incrementalist politics, and the ascendancy of a bipartisan technocratic elite in both the Democratic and Republican Parties that has been accelerating the concentration of power in the hands of an increasingly small number of mega corporations and institutions.

We believe that it's time to get back to big organizing in a big way. It's already happening, as evidenced not only by the Bernie Sanders campaign but also by other campaigns and movements before it, such as Obama in 2008, Occupy Wall Street, the effort to unseat George W. Bush in 2003–2004. We also see it in the immigration movement (in particular the Dreamers), the movement to defend black lives, and to some degree in movements on the right such as the campaign of Ron Paul in 2004, the rise of the Tea Party, and even some elements of the madness that was the Trump campaign.

Big organizing is what leaders do in movements that mobilize millions of people.

Not everyone in these movements is a leader, but in big organizing, volunteer leaders emerge by the thousands from every classroom, family, office and work area, neighborhood, and prison block. The movement doesn't need to awaken or even train them—these leaders emerge ready to make change, and they bring their full selves and life experience to the task of building a movement that works. Our families, workplaces, schools, social networks, and other institutions are all inherently political. And in the current social context, people don't need to be awakened politically—they are ready to get to work to make change.

A movement powered by big organizing provides these already existing leaders with a scalable way to make a difference that evolves and becomes more sophisticated and powerful over time. On the Bernie campaign, this looked like volunteer leaders holding phone-banking parties, staging volunteer canvasses, and holding volunteer-led mass organizing meetings. In other movement contexts, volunteer leaders would take on different "rinse and repeat" tasks.

The point is not that the revolution will be phone-banked but that the revolution will be led by volunteer leaders who take on the work of a campaign plan, a plan that is so big it can only be accomplished when everyone who wants change (a majority of the people) works together. This could be everyone on a campus, in a community, in a workplace or industry, or in the entire country.

In big organizing, leaders operate with a high level of autonomy and creativity while all working toward the same, centrally determined, shared goal. Sometimes that shared goal is decided upon by a central movement leadership and sometimes it is presented by the circumstances of history.

The team we assembled on the Bernie Sanders campaign, which came to be called the "distributed organizing team," believed that we had to do whatever was in our power to support and grow the volunteer Bernie movement. Not only was this going to be crucial to helping Bernie win, but it was also one of our best hopes of jump-starting a resurgence of big organizing in America.

The Bernie campaign gave us a glimpse of what is possible. When Bernie called for a political revolution, the call was answered—improbably to some—by hundreds of thousands of volunteers who went to work building a voter contact machine the likes of which has never been seen in a presidential primary. This was truly big organizing. As it turned out, people were just waiting to be asked to do something big to win something big. Defying the conventional wisdom, the Bernie campaign demonstrated that the organizing sector has reached a dramatic tipping point.

The Bernie phenomenon was even more surprising because over the past two decades most organizing at the presidential campaign level was based staunchly on small organizing. Campaign staff used data and technology to "microtarget" tiny slices of the electorate in the hopes that winning these segments would add up to a narrow majority. Once elected, these politicians promised to achieve incremental change via mundane policy tweaks. In return, they asked for only minimal participation from the people being organized.

Small organizing drives a negative feedback loop where fewer and fewer people participate because the changes promised are too small to be worth anyone's time, leading campaigners in turn to lower their expectations of participation. Even though campaigners and policy makers are the drivers of this process, they experience it as proof of the apathy of the people. The result is that too many elected officials are basing important decisions not on what would be best for all Americans but on what they imagine would appeal to a small number of swing voters usually at the center-right of the political debate.

On the road back to big organizing, there have been some earnest attempts, fascinating experiments, and false starts. We thought we had seen big organizing emerge via digital advocacy groups that emerged in the decade following the (stolen) election of George W. Bush. These groups built huge email lists that could be contacted to raise money, collect petition signatures, or gather people together to attend protests. The organizations themselves, often with no brick-and-mortar offices, operated with small staffs and low overheads.

But the task of the staff of digital organizations (more often than not) was less about organizing the people on the other side of the emails and more about managing the list. There were some exceptions. CREDO was a bit of a unicorn: a mobile phone company that raised tens of millions of dollars for progressive groups, many of which do on-the-ground organizing. MoveOn.org raised a lot of money for candidates. And in some extraordinary moments, groups like CREDO moved in the direction of big organizing. For example, CREDO SuperPAC opened offices to help volunteers defeat Tea Party congressmen in 2012 and launched the Pledge of Resistance, organizing nearly one hundred thousand people to pledge to risk arrest to stop the Keystone XL pipeline. At the time of this writing, MoveOn.org is launching volunteer canvasses at a large scale for the 2016 general election for the first time in its history. But looking at the field more broadly, in large part, digital advocacy groups' experiments have been limited and much more measured.

That all changed when the distributed organizing program of the Bernie campaign embraced a big organizing approach. A small hybrid team of super volunteers and professional organizers took a list of emails and phone numbers and a suite of consumer software supplemented with custom coding and built a new mass organization made up of thousands of volunteer teams with accountable leadership and measurable impact on the campaign's aggressive goals.

This successful marriage of digital campaigning and volunteer field efforts in Bernie's distributed organizing combined aspects of old-school organizing practices with the social platforms that provide nearly constant mediation of the way people live and work in contemporary society. It set down a new marker for organizing: harnessing a powerful, tech-enabled, people-powered model that is infinitely scalable and poses a potent threat to the status quo.

The Bernie campaign showed America that there could be another way. The big organizing that was the hallmark of the Bernie volunteer movement seeks to turn out big majorities in support of big ideas by integrating new disruptive technology into the practice of political organizing. Small organizing works well enough when incumbents want to maintain the status quo, but it isn't big enough to challenge the establishment. Technology is now continuously revolutionizing daily life. When organizers figure out how to integrate the huge opportunities that new, social technology provides with effective peer-to-peer organizing principles and practices as part of a smart, centralized plan—that's big organizing. And it's the way we can win the political revolution—whether it's in a big national fight to take control of government or in a series of meaningful local fights leading to victories that matter.

Big organizing isn't just about the effective use of the newest technology to scale participation in politics. At the most fundamental level, big organizing is how we create campaigns that allow people to work together to realize their dreams for a more just world.

Big organizing is big in more ways than one. We have to have a meaningful message and big goals. Instead of asking for the change that politicians think is possible, we have to ask for the change that is actually needed to solve problems. This will necessarily be big.

In big organizing we have big target universes. We need to talk to everyone—not just narrow slices of assumed swing voters—about what we want to achieve. We have to get as many people as possible engaged in the work of talking with voters. We have to have voters make demands of their representatives in Congress. Together, we will constitute a wave that will swamp the influence of big money, corporate media, and other establishment players who are invested in maintaining the status quo.

What do big organizing goals look like? Make public college free. End the drug war and stop the mass incarceration of black and brown people. Let everyone enroll in Medicare and make health care truly universal. Pursue an industrial policy that seeks to put everyone to work in the best jobs possible. None of these are crazy things to ask for. And it's not crazy to ask for them all at once. In fact, all of those things are the status quo in almost every high- and middle-income country in the world. Bernie Sanders called for them, and he almost won the presidential primary. Our problems are big, so our solutions must be big as well. To achieve them we need a new kind of organizing, and that is big organizing.

Big organizing rarely works around a single issue. Our struggles are all connected. We can't achieve universal health care until we have immigration reform. We can't fix income equality until we deal with structural racism and the historical legacy of slavery. We can't resolve national and global security issues or reach full employment without working as hard as possible to stop climate change. Big organizing also needs to have a clear and credible theory of change that explains why organizing matters. Bernie's message was that if we wanted to win on all of the issues, we had to organize for a political revolution.

So how do we talk to everybody about our big ideas? Part of the answer is to leverage technology to talk to everyone and allow thousands to scale up into leadership roles. What that looks like is a volunteer-driven campaign with consumer software—connected by custom coding—at the center; this structure makes it possible to scale the participation of people doing sophisticated work on central plans.

Small organizing candidate campaigns depend on so-called "big data" to narrow the number of people that must be engaged with predictive modeling, micro targeting, and message testing and segmentation. Big organizing depends on technology as well, but it emphasizes a very different approach. Big organizing uses technology platforms—particularly free, consumer-oriented, social collaboration tools—to get as many people as possible engaged in executing a campaign plan and to enable those people to talk to each other and to as many voters as possible regardless of where the volunteers live or how much time they have to spend doing it each week.

In big organizing, volunteers act as the staff of the campaign. With a structure where leadership roles at nearly every level are primarily filled by volunteers, a campaign can scale up with everyone doing more and more valuable work at every level.

In contrast, a campaign that only engages volunteers in basic tasks breaks down if there's a huge influx of people willing to help. For example, if too many volunteers show up for Get Out The Vote (GOTV), organizers run out of walk packets. Too often, they'll send the extra volunteers to hold signs on street corners or some equally worthless task that won't impact the outcome of the election. Big organizing demands a structure that scales. And this structure requires the ability to absorb and delegate work to volunteers at all management levels as the campaign grows.

In our corner of the Bernie campaign, we attempted to build a big organizing structure capable of accommodating limitless numbers of volunteers by combining technology with old-school, peer-to-peer organizing. The result was a national volunteer apparatus capable of distributing the work to hundreds of thousands of volunteers, giving a large number of people leadership roles, holding people accountable, and making it efficient for people to engage in high-impact voter contact no matter where they lived.

These volunteers worked in teams. The teams were led by volunteers who had proved themselves to be effective and accountable through work. It was the primary responsibility of campaign staff to recruit, empower, and grow these volunteer teams until the campaign scaled to the size necessary to win the big changes we sought.

This may sound daunting to actually accomplish, given the big numbers of people necessary to make it work well enough to win. The good news is that people are waiting for you to ask them to do something big. What we've learned from the Bernie campaign and many other movements is that far more people are willing to step up if you ask them to do something big to win something big than they would be if you asked them to do something small to win something small.

In some ways, big organizing is what populists used to simply call organizing but with the potential for much greater scale thanks to new and accessible technology for connecting people. But how did the progressive movement—including leading populists—become so focused on small organizing? To answer that, we need to introduce you to someone named Saul Alinsky and the style of community organizing that he popularized.

Saul Alinsky got his start in the shadow of the mass industrial labor movement of the 1930s. While working on his PhD in sociology in the low-income Back of the Yards neighborhood of Chicago, he participated in the birth of a community organization led by priests and other neighborhood leaders. With support from the Catholic Church and major, corporate-funded foundations, Alinsky hired organizers to launch community organizations in other cities, and eventually he formed a training school for community organizers and wrote books on his philosophy of organizing, including the now classic *Rules for Radicals*.

At the heart of Alinsky's methods was the one-on-one personal relationship between the organizer and the subject who was to be organized. Through one-on-one conversations, regular people were to be enlightened to their disempowered lot by a charismatic super organizer who came in from outside of the community. In theory, the organizer gradually activated community members and built what's called a mass power organization, the purpose of which was to move people from despair to action in small steps—climbing what the digital organizing generation would later call "the ladder of engagement"—and then to create disruptive campaigns that brought powerful forces to a bargaining table where the organizer could negotiate for incremental victories.

Rules for Radicals, which he published in 1971, encapsulates this organizing philosophy. Some of these rules are tactical and helpful to any activist, such as "A good tactic is one your people enjoy," and "The threat is usually more terrifying than the thing itself," and "Pick the target, freeze it, personalize it, and polarize it."

But other parts of his philosophy are more problematic. For all the things Alinsky got right, he was explicitly looking to outflank the populist movement of his time and provide an alternative that was more palatable to the liberal elite. His funders were particularly eager to form incrementalist black and Latino organizations that would absorb, manage, and redirect the anger that was expressing itself beginning in the 1950s through urban uprisings. Alinsky disparaged the idea of revolutionary change and explicitly sought to undermine black, Latino, and working class revolutionary movements.

Alinsky believed that the purpose of building power was not to put the people in power, but to compel negotiation. He wanted to win a seat at the 1950's and 1960's establishment tables for the poor and disenfranchised. Part of the reason this seemed like a reasonable strategy to so many good people was that, at the time, the table was overflowing. Surely there was enough for everyone! His vision of constant campaigning was aimed at recruiting members into an organization and keeping them engaged as a noisy army that an organizer could then leverage to win as many table scraps as possible. It didn't matter what the controversy was, just that it kept people engaged.

Alinsky's approach was premised on the paternalistic concept that an enlightened core of outside organizers was necessary first to show the poor that there was a better way and then to represent them in a battle with elites. *Rules for Radicals* contains sample dialogues between organizers and poor people that would make most people today cringe.

It might seem strange that we're spending so much time talking about a guy that many of our readers have probably never heard of, but hundreds of important organizations were founded by organizers that Alinsky hired, trained, or influenced. When we explored the backgrounds of electoral and labor organizers, we found that many of the most influential got their start with an Alinsky-descended organization. The Alinsky model simply became the standard for the entire liberal and progressive world. But it's time to move on.

The big organizing model that can fuel revolutions believes that communities are filled with talented and intelligent people who understand what is broken and, when given material and strategic resources, can wrest power from elites and make lasting change. A political revolution is different from community organizing as we know it today.

Alinsky wrote rules for radicals. In this book, we offer rules for revolutionaries to help you learn new tactics and strategies for building a political revolution.

You Won't Get a Revolution If You Don't Ask for One

★ becky & zack ★

P eople are waiting for you to ask them to do something big. Movements require clear demands for solutions as radical as our problems, and you need authentic, credible leaders to deliver the message.

What set Bernie apart from the start of his campaign was his message and his authenticity as a messenger. Then he unleashed the makings of a real political revolution—he asked for one.

He outlined the radical solutions our moment calls for, not the tepid incrementalist compromises that most politicians think are all that is feasible.

Bernie didn't talk about education tax credits or even debt-free college. He demanded free college tuition.

He didn't advocate for complicated health insurance schemes, he said "health care is a human right."

Bernie called for an end to mass incarceration, not incremental changes in sentencing law.

He had no ten-point plan to regulate fracking to the point that it wouldn't be feasible in most places in the United States. He simply said we should ban fracking.

When it came to the deportation of children, he couldn't have been clearer. "I will not deport children from the United States of America," he said.

Part of Bernie's effectiveness came from his matter-of-fact way of speaking and his old-school Brooklyn accent. But what really allowed people to trust him is that "he has been saying the same thing for thirty years." Bernie volunteers said that everywhere we went.

People ask us: What can *we* learn from the big organizing that powered the volunteer movement behind Bernie Sanders? Is it only possible in a presidential campaign?

No. Think about the movement to defend black lives. Leaders like Alicia Garza and Erica Garner are powerful messengers with a powerful message. Who they are and what they are saying and where they are saying it represents a major change from how national civil rights advocacy has been voiced and led in the past few decades. Or think about climate activists fighting to keep fossil fuels in the ground. Native American leaders, ranchers, and students are leading these fights instead of the public interest lawyers whom the mainstream green movement has had leading the charge on environmental issues. These new leaders are showing the world that the fight to keep fossil fuels in the ground is not a pet issue; it is no less than a basic struggle for human rights.

In fact, people are willing to go big to win big change. When there is a credible plan to win something truly game changing, more people commit to actions, big and small, to work together toward victory.

In 2011, CREDO was one of a handful of groups that joined 350.org in organizing mass arrests at the White House. Becky had already been deeply involved in the fight to stop the Keystone XL pipeline, but organizing civil disobedience was an escalation of tactics.

Elijah Zarlin, who had worked in the Chicago headquarters of President Obama's 2008 campaign and at the time worked for CREDO, wrote an email to CREDO's members. The email began, "This isn't an everyday request. I'd like you to consider doing something really big."

That big thing was to go to jail in peaceful civil disobedience to send a message to the president to reject a tar sands oil pipeline. Keystone XL wasn't just any pipeline, it was the fuse on a veritable carbon bomb lying below the surface of western Canada—oil that we had to keep in the ground.

When Elijah was arrested in front of the White House with over a hundred other protesters (including Becky), he had to sit for hours in the hot August sun in a white dress shirt and the tie he had last worn on Election Day in 2008 celebrating his team's historic win—a win that put the man he was now protesting into the White House. Sitting next to him was a middle-aged businessman sweating in a blazer too heavy for the heat. (Protesters had all been asked to dress in their Sunday school best so their image would be more "Middle America" than "hippie forest defender.")

"How did you end up here?" Elijah asked.

The man replied that he had received an email inviting him. Without revealing his identity, Elijah pressed, "From what group?"

The man couldn't remember. "I'm on a lot of lists," he said. "But I do remember opening the email and reading the first line. It said, 'I'm going to ask you to do something big.' And I thought to myself, I'm ready to do something big to stop climate change."

Hours after the arrests, after a sweaty police van ride to Anacostia, where the protestors were processed and later released, Elijah looked up his co-arrestee in the CREDO database. The man had never signed a petition. Never. But when he got an email asking him to do something big, he drove to DC, put on a blazer and tie and sat down in front of the White House and refused to move until the police arrested him and he was carted away.

CREDO went on to organize the Pledge of Resistance in 2013 and nearly one hundred thousand people pledged to risk arrest in order to defend the climate and block the Keystone XL pipeline. With help from direct-action trainers, Rainforest Action Network, and other allies, they went around the country training teams of volunteers to plan actions in their communities—at TransCanada offices, at US State Department offices, and at local Democratic Party headquarters.

We're not saying you can just ask people to do anything big and they'll do it. That's absolutely not it! Here are the rules behind the rule.

First, the goal you're asking people to spend their precious time on needs to be worth their while. Remember, people are struggling every day at their jobs or their schools, in their neighborhoods, and sometimes in their families. Why should they join your fight? If you win, is it going to make a difference for them personally, or for their children or grandchildren, or for their community or country? Your big ask needs to be big in the real lives of the people you're asking to join you. It's not enough that you believe it's big.

Second, you need to be able to tell people about a plan that gets from the world as it is to the world where you've won. And that plan needs to be credible. People are smart and, for good reason, are increasingly cynical when it comes to sussing out plans that will never work. They've seen countless political failures in their lives—personally, locally, and nationally. Your big ask needs to make sense to them.

Finally, you need to offer people a way to participate that will truly make a difference. And again, people are super smart about sensing when they're being given busy work. Moreover, you need to give people small, medium, and really big ways to contribute—because some people will be able to put in a lot of time, and many more will only have one day per month or a couple of afternoons per week. If people see that you're able to give everyone a way to participate, this makes your plan more credible (which helps win over more people) and allows you to take full advantage of all the people who are available to help—which is what's going to propel you to win!

Any campaign, no matter the size, can ask people to do something big if it's working toward something people believe is worth fighting for.

So the key to big organizing is that you don't just ask people to pay staff at an organization to do something big (though supporting some staff with small dollar contributions is part of it). You ask people to be part of that something big. Because doing something big is only possible if everyone is doing it together. And that takes a lot of work. You need supporters to do big things (and a lot of small things that add up to big things) to help you execute a plan to win big change.

Almost anyone can make a big ask. You don't have to be charismatic to make a big ask. You just have to have an ask that is worth working for, a plan to win, and meaningful roles for volunteers. The ask should never be for volunteers to add their names to a list so that organizers might call them back later; it needs to be immediate and crucial.

This is not something we're discovering but rather something we're lifting up. Every day movements are doing big organizing in the local context—and some movements in a lot of local contexts, and a few in a national context! They understand that people are less and less inclined to take small actions in isolation for small gains. Especially when our problems are so big, and it's gotten so bad, and everybody knows it.

Hillary Clinton's primary campaign struggled to get a handful of events planned by volunteers on her website when Bernie had thousands. On January 25, 2016, just a week before the Iowa caucus, a Bernie supporter on Reddit pulled the number of public events listed on map.berniesanders.com and www.hillaryclinton.com/events for within a 250-mile range of New York City, Chicago, Los Angeles, and Austin. The Clinton campaign had 39 phone banks listed. The Bernie campaign had 1,809.

While Bernie was explaining that he needed tens of millions of people to get involved in the fight for justice and was inviting his supporters to build a political revolution, the Clinton campaign was sending out emails that said "make three calls today, and when Hillary wins the Iowa caucuses tomorrow night, you'll feel great knowing you helped make history."

People didn't want to do even small things for the small changes that Clinton promised. They understood that to actually help "make history" it takes more than making three calls. The good news for organizers who want to help build the political revolution is that people really are just waiting for you to ask them to do something big. So ask.

This might be our favorite rule. Because it's also how we ended up on the Bernie campaign together. Zack gave up a promising new business to join the Bernie campaign. Becky gave up her job running CREDO Action, something she had spent fifteen years building, and joined him. Some people thought we were nuts. We accepted giant pay cuts and took on work that usually was done by more junior people. But this was a chance to do something big to win something big. Bernie made the big ask, inviting people to come together and build a political revolution. We were ready to answer that call and ended up doing something bigger than we ever imagined.

The Revolution Will Not Be Handed to You on a Silver Platter

★ zack ★

The revolution is not something you order to your own specifications. You have to take the obstacles with the opportunities. And oftentimes it's amid chaos that you find the best conditions for introducing radical innovations.

When I arrived in Washington, DC, to start work on the Bernie campaign, I thought I had set my expectations low enough. After all, I had worked on two incredibly dysfunctional presidential campaigns—Howard Dean and then John Kerry. And I had the impression that the Bernie campaign was going to be even crazier. I thought I was not only prepared for the worst, I was actually looking forward to the pandemonium. It is only smack in the middle of maximum chaos that radical innovation has a chance.

I was eager to put my experience to work, and I wondered if it would make things better or worse that most of the staff—including the campaign manager and national field director—had no presidential campaign experience. From the outset, the campaign was cautious and cheap. I had been told that Bernie was wary of being left in debt—which seemed absurd to those of us who knew that hundreds of millions of dollars were going to pour in through the online small-dollar fundraising operation.

Getting the campaign to hire any new staff outside of Iowa and New Hampshire had been like pulling teeth according to the folks already there. The opening that allowed me to squeeze into the campaign was a planned nationwide wave of distributed kickoff events. There was no staffer available on the tiny campaign team with the time and experience to pull something like that off. And yet the July 29th events had already been announced—there was no going back. They needed someone to run them, and I had been doing these distributed events since 2000.

I wasn't worried about the campaign being cheap. I was sure that the plan I was going to pitch for grassroots organizing in the later states would be much smaller than what they were expecting me to ask for. To start off, we just needed a handful of initial staff, a little money for online tools, a software developer, and a lean travel budget—because we were going to have to build a nearly all volunteer-led movement if we were going to have a chance of electing Bernie Sanders president.

But on my very first day in DC, I fell into depression as I learned from my friends Tim Tagaris, Michael Whitney, and Scott Goodstein that the campaign was basically not hiring *anyone*—except field organizers in Iowa and New Hampshire—and that there were no solid plans to do so at any time in the future.

The people already assembled were amazing pros. Kenneth Pennington, Bernie's twenty-four-year-old digital director, was ultimately responsible for the stable of digital talent. Tim Tagaris, a partner at Revolution Messaging, would lead a digital fundraising team that would defy expectations and eventually, to the shock of the nation, make Bernie financially competitive in a race that nearly everyone expected to be a Hillary Clinton coronation. Michael Whitney, an incredible digital strategist whom I first met on the Dean campaign when he was only nineteen, was Tim's deputy. They were working under the auspices of Revolution Messaging's founder, Scott Goodstein, and its creative director, Arun Chaudry. But still, this shocking news was nearly impossible to assimilate.

And so it was that on my very first day I was beginning to lose my mind and getting rapidly grumpier and then flat out angry. By the evening of my first day in DC, I found myself begging Scott, Tim, Michael, and Arun to march with me to tell Bernie how big of a missed opportunity this was and to plead with him to fix it. But they had already pushed as hard as anyone could for more resources and faster progress. They couldn't keep banging their heads against the wall and eventually had had to accept the reality of the campaign— which is exactly what they were insisting I do—or get out of town.

"This is a crime against history," I said. "We're allowing the biggest opportunity for change in one hundred years to be thrown away."

Arun told me I needed to chill out and began to get visibly annoyed. I was marginalizing myself on Day 1. I realized it was time to go sleep on it, or I was going to blow up and make enemies of everyone there and an embarrassment of myself. I fell asleep hopeless.

I woke up filled with excitement. I had been shooting my mouth off for two decades about how mass movements were supposed to be run by the people, not by mercenaries, and how there were more and better leaders among a movement's supporters than a movement could ever hope to hire. I had been lulled into a permanent dependence on staffers while working with big nonprofits and campaigns. Now I, of all people, was wondering how we were going to have the revolution without first filling out a bunch of W-4 forms.

It hit me that this extreme situation that Bernie had forced on us was the only way we'd ever get to do this. And this is one of the many reasons I appreciate and am forever grateful to Bernie for being Bernie and not letting anyone talk him into being a typical presidential candidate. Bernie was forcing us to rely almost 100 percent on the volunteer leadership that was already out there—among all the hundreds of local Bernie groups, many of whom were already months old, and the tens of thousands of people who had already signed up to help.

Don't get me wrong: We could have moved faster and done more with bigger and earlier investments in basic staff and infrastructure. It would be months before the campaign paid for the voter file for the whole country and a phone bank dialer, let alone teams to train volunteers how to use them. We would be constantly hamstrung by lack of staff who could have worked with volunteers to open offices, to print and distribute materials, and to accept all manner of in-kind donations and assistance.

But the revolution is not something you order to your own specifications. You have to take the obstacles with the opportunities. There is no provider of revolutionary conditions whose job it is to set everything up just right for you. The greatest opportunities—like the lack of focus on the later states that would allow us to utilize volunteers at the same level as staff—went hand in hand with the obstacle of the campaign's inability to give us resources until months after we first needed them (if at all).

The opportunity I most wanted was to be on the front lines with the people building this new way to scale a people-powered campaign. To be free to do that, I really needed someone who was passionate, creative, and a deep thinker about organizing, who could help build the program while interacting with the campaign at a senior level and ensure that we had the budget, buy in, and leadership. That person—if I could somehow convince the campaign to hire her—was an organizer with experience in volunteer-driven antiestablishment campaigns, Claire Sandberg.

The antifracking campaign in New York that Claire helped organize was led by fierce volunteers from the state's southern tier counties, volunteers who refused to follow the direction of the more seasoned professional environmental campaigners working at New York City–based nonprofits. Claire had a visceral understanding that plenty of volunteers can sometimes work just as hard, with the same passion and focus on winning, as professional staffers, if they can just be brought into the fold. That was exactly the orientation the campaign would need if we were going to build a fifty-state distributed strategy in the primary and have to staff it almost entirely with volunteers.

So I asked the campaign manager, Jeff Weaver, if I could be brought on as a senior advisor and suggested he hire Claire into the digital organizing director role the campaign was initially talking to me about. I explained that what they were asking me to do was more than a full-time job. I knew Claire wanted on the campaign and was ready to come immediately. Jeff agreed, with a little bit of ambiguity and no details. I was surprised and grateful.

Claire and I got started right away sending out a series of emails asking the Bernie email list who on the list was willing to take on larger roles than typically are filled by volunteers, and sending subsequent messages designed to narrow down the pool. In the end we still had tens of thousands who said they were ready to essentially drop everything to do whatever we asked 24/7. This was too many people for us to process, of course—and one of our terrible regrets on the campaign was that so many thousands of people were left underutilized until we finally had scalable meaningful asks that anyone could take and run with. There is a catch-22 when it comes to engaging volunteers on a campaign that starts with virtually no staff: You can't engage the volunteers because you haven't onboarded volunteers to engage them! We had to simply put the thousands of volunteers who were dying to get started out of our minds as we began with the first handful.

We started working at this point with Hector Sigala, who not only oversaw all of Bernie's social media accounts but was also incredibly the campaign's IT manager. Kenneth and Hector were our heroes for allowing us to start sending emails and working with data before either of us were officially employed, which they knew would take several weeks or possibly months to happen. They took a leap of faith—coaxed along by Tim, who endorsed all the things that we were doing that seemed crazy to anyone who had never seen them before. Kenneth, like any rational person would, needed all of this crazy stuff explained—for example, the very idea that thousands of people who we had never met would organize semiofficial public events for the campaign. In meetings, I felt like jumping out the window whenever Kenneth grilled me over all of the details, but he was one of the central figures who made Bernie's rise possible, and I was reminded that back in 2003, when MoveOn.org was inventing a lot of this stuff, it was twenty-two-year-old inexperienced Eli Pariser who played a critical role.

Recruited through email and over social media, thousands of volunteers across the country were preparing for the July 29th kickoff events. Using conference calls, one-on-one calls, local Slack teams, and plain old email threads, we organized teams in several cities that were going to attempt to go beyond house parties to hold large public events.

We did not have field staff in any of the big cities outside of Iowa and New Hampshire to help pull off large events, but we had at least dozens of people in every large city who had responded "Yes!" to our request for organizers who wanted to organize events at local pubs, theaters, and community centers. With so little time in between the millions of details we had to attend to at that early stage, we did something totally unorthodox that we knew probably wouldn't work: We sent email threads to groups of volunteers in a few dozen cities, letting them know that there were only two of us responsible for forty-six states and therefore we had little time to help them, but asking them to get together and start organizing events in large venues on their own. I experimented in each thread with a different set of instructions and said, "Good luck!"

Over the next couple of weeks, the number of events continued to shoot up. But in addition to a hundred mundane yet vexing problems, we had several really big problems that could still jeopardize the July 29th events. To address each one, I began to establish teams of high-functioning volunteers as Claire valiantly navigated our way through the tightly packed, chaotic, and erratic campaign bureaucracy, shepherding our interactions with the press team, early state staff, Bernie's office, advance, and so on.

The first problem was that www.berniesanders.com was receiving dozens of emails per day from volunteers with questions about the July 29th events—questions like "How do I connect my laptop to my television so that I can show the livestream of Bernie?" and "What time is the livestream?" even though we had put the time in all twenty-five emails we had sent to them about it—in addition to thousands of general emails about everything from Bernie's policies and strategy to requests to donate. These emails were read by interns in the Burlington, Vermont, headquarters—interns who would then stand up and go looking for people to solve the volunteers' problems. Because the Burlington office was so small, with so few staffers at the time, they would wind up in the office of national field director Phil Fiermonte or of campaign manager Jeff Weaver himself.

One of the things that was causing so much consternation among volunteers, and generating so many angry emails that made their way to Jeff, was that the map tool on our website that people used to find events to attend crashed whenever we sent an email out pointing to it. We were charged with signing up as many attendees as possible to now more than one thousand events—but each time we emailed to ask people to attend, the tool that would allow them to do so virtually disappeared!

All of these problems came to a head when Jeff sat Claire and I down to bring up concerns that he and other leaders had because of all the emails and even phone calls that were coming in. In addition to the chatter in Burlington, the field organizers in Iowa and New Hampshire were confused about what we were doing, and it was messing with their plans. And they had a right to be angry. Because the campaign had no central coordination, they had been totally left out of the loop about the July 29th events plan.

When you do this kind of distributed organizing, there is always a bit of chaos out there. There are always a handful of volunteers who need a lot of special attention—and always a few who will never be happy no matter how much attention you give them. Everywhere else I've done this sort of work, this has always been accepted as part of the deal of being big and distributed, and everyone has been okay with it. The only way to manage such a sprawling campaign with such a tiny team is by not worrying about those edge cases.

On the Bernie campaign, this wasn't possible. Part of it was the massive scale of the organizing—we had so many event hosts that the number who were having problems was inevitably large. And they all seemed to know how to reach the campaign manager and national field director directly by email. At the beginning of the campaign, sometimes they even used an email address that Bernie himself checked.

So we had to provide a higher level of service to our event hosts—but who would provide it? And how would we solve these vexing tech problems when there was no budget for developers? We knew complaining about a lack of resources and staff was not an option. I had a sinking feeling that we might already be losing our chance to lead grassroots organizing before we had barely gotten started. After all, when all this was going down, Claire and I had still not been formally hired, let alone paid. The staff in Burlington, including the CFO, didn't even know we existed.

It was a terrible situation in which to be trying to make a revolutionary breakthrough. But I reminded myself once more that the revolution is not delivered on a silver platter. It comes in a chaotic mess of bureaucracy, inexperience, confusion, and contradiction. And this made me realize that I had waited too long to start putting the campaign into the hands of those volunteers whose faces I had seen on my first morning of the campaign a week and a half earlier. I had thought we would wait until after July 29th to start building teams to help us build out a volunteer-run national organizing program. But the revolution was here, and though the conditions could not have been worse for recruiting, onboarding, and training volunteers, it was time!

The Revolution Will Not Be Staffed

★ zack ★

There will never be enough money to pay all the organizers the revolution needs. The good news is there are more than enough amazing volunteer leaders among the people, and three or four talented and committed volunteers working part time can often do the work of a full-time paid staffer. When you've got at least a handful of people committed to a cause signed up on a list, you've got what you need to kick-start a vibrant organization.

Most hard work gets done by teams. In the world of organizing, the 2008 Obama primary popularized the strategy of forming "neighborhood teams." A detail often forgotten about the historic 2008 race was that Obama was far behind in the polls in South Carolina, including with African American voters, for most of the race. Obama's South Carolina staff in the primary, led by Jeremy Bird, organized hundreds of teams over more than a year of preparation to win the election block by block, neighbor by neighbor.

Harvard professor Marshall Ganz, working with Joy Cushman, who would later join Obama's South Carolina campaign, had rolled out a team model to Sierra Club chapters in an experimental project the year before. The model made its way to the Obama campaign via Joy and Jeremy, who had been students of Marshall while at Harvard. This model got a lot of attention in and after 2008 and it's come by many to be called the "snowflake model" because, in trainings, Marshall and the Obama organizers he mentored showed volunteers a snowflake-like diagram representing a team, with a leader in the center, and lines coming off the leader who were team members.

In the 2008 Obama model, every team was formed by a paid staff organizer. The basic "rinse and repeat" cycle of work for an Obama organizer under Jeremy's model was the identification, recruitment, and training of a neighborhood team leader; the eventual formation of a new neighborhood team by that leader; and then the practice of holding leaders accountable for continued production.

In Ohio, the state that Jeremy ran during the general election, and in several other states, this cycle was developed into both an art and a science. The Obama Ohio headquarters was larger than Bernie's national headquarters. More than one hundred staffers worked mostly in efficient silence until suddenly someone rang a bell hanging from the wall near Jeremy's desk. Everyone dropped what they were doing and applauded and cheered—until the ringing became so routine that it was met with only an obligatory hoot from somewhere in the room. The bell indicated that a new team leader somewhere in the state had just agreed to lead.

The structure that emerged from this kind of organizing was like a one-snowflake-thick layer of snow covering all of Ohio and several other battleground states in 2008, with each team having been created by and reporting to a paid staff organizer.

The purpose of these teams was to do all kinds of effective voter contact work. The teams received guidance from the paid organizers who managed them, but also took care of a lot of the local strategy on their own. They knew their neighborhoods best! This was the beauty of the neighborhood team model. It was an effective system because the teams had the freedom, trust, and respect of the campaign to work their neighborhood in the best way they could—with plenty of guidance, tools, and training from the campaign.

The success of teams could be measured in voter contacts produced and recorded in the campaign's voter database, known in campaign shorthand as VAN (Voter Activation Network). The campaign had a central plan, the work was distributed into teams, and every team had a staff supervisor. The slogan of the Obama 2008 field campaign was "Respect. Include. Empower." In Jeremy's office and in most of the Obama offices you could see those words in big letters somewhere on the walls.

The neighborhood team model had a limitation, however: It could only scale in proportion to the number of paid staff—each team had to be created and overseen by a paid staffer. Each of the verbs in the command "Respect. Include. Empower." were sandwiched between a subject and an object. The actors were paid field organizers. The acted upon were volunteers.

This worked fine for the battleground states in Obama's 2008 general election run in large part because only a dozen states were in play and they had tens of millions of dollars available to pay staff to blanket those states with that thin layer of snowflakes. And in the primaries, the snowflake model was really only tried in earnest in South Carolina. The primary campaign didn't have enough money to massively staff all the states at the level required by the model. No presidential primary campaign, including Obama's, both of Clinton's, and Bernie's, has ever had the resources to do that—and it's unlikely one ever will.

What keen political observers learned in the protracted, fifty-state Obama–Clinton battle of 2008 was that a primary campaign could stay competitive all the way to the bitter end. Every state matters! Even every territory! In other words, the primary of 2016 called for a new fifty-state model that could somehow respect, include, and *unleash* volunteer leaders in a whole new way.

So on the Bernie campaign, we knew that we needed teams—because that was the only way to get large numbers of people doing work without direct supervision by paid staff that we knew would arrive in many states only days or weeks before the elections. We needed a process in which our campaign could somehow mass produce thousands of snowflakes very quickly—a snowmaking machine! We eventually figured out how to do this most efficiently with the mass meetings we called barnstorms. But the barnstorm program was a huge, complex operation that required many large and sophisticated volunteer teams to run. Back at the beginning of July, we didn't even have *one* team—it was just Claire and me, and forty-six states.

We knew we weren't going to be able to hire hundreds of people. We weren't sure if we would be able to hire *any* people. So we had to build our central operation out of volunteers. How could we go from two people to hundreds in such a short time? And how could those hundreds be structured into a productive organization of interlocking volunteer teams?

By July, the Bernie movement had reached a fever pitch. Leaders of local groups and hundreds of individuals who were desperate to get involved in the unstaffed states had figured out that Claire and I were the staffers responsible for organizing them. Checking my email or voice-mail or looking at my texts was like peeking into a stadium filled with an angry mob—and they were all angry at *us*! And justifiably. Every single one of them was saying—some more politely than others—"Don't you see that if you idiots put us to work effectively, there are enough of us to win this election?" I did see it. And it killed me. I could barely sleep in those first couple of months, I frequently woke up nauseous, and I sometimes felt dizzy during the day. It wasn't that I was overworked—I'm plenty experienced with campaign hours. I was sick over the huge opportunity we were letting slip away with each passing day—the opportunity to *start* an actual revolution and change everything by winning this damn election.

And this, for me and Becky—who, at that point, had yet to come on board but with whom I was talking to frequently—is what it was all about: Could the Bernie movement, in the vast expanse of the inevitably unstaffed primary states, show that a revolutionary mass movement was not only possible, but could kick ass?

We needed to start rolling a snowball.

If you didn't grow up in a snowy place, then you won't remember that feeling of rolling a giant snowball on the first sticky snowfall of winter. You start by simply packing a little snow in between your hands. Then you start rolling that little snowball on the ground, and new snow sticks right to it. Minutes later, you've got a serious snowball going. The beauty of it is that once you get the snowball started, all you have to do is push. If there's a hill in your yard, you can push a snowball until it's as tall as your eight-year-old self. Without a hill, you may need a few of your friends. After you've pushed the snowball over every square foot of the neighborhood, you could have a snowball approaching the size of a giant boulder. And then someone's mom takes a picture.

That's kind of how it went in July as we created volunteer teams to solve the problems that were emerging in the run up to July 29th.

While Claire was busy setting up the July 29th kickoff inside the campaign and working to convince the campaign leadership that our department even deserved to exist, I got busy creating teams to handle the immediate needs we had as we organized toward the 2,700 distributed organizing events.

One volunteer team led to another. First came the help desk. We emailed a handful of volunteers who had said they were ready to take on special challenges, and asked them to staff a volunteer email help desk—to answer the questions and deal with the problems coming in from all volunteers, especially the ones who needed help with their July 29th event and who were causing such headaches in Burlington. One great benefit of this was that volunteers would be better served, but the real necessity was so that we could stop exposing the campaign manager of a national presidential campaign to the trials and tribulations of volunteers struggling to connect their computers to their televisions or understand the differences between time zones.

I kicked off the team by inviting them onto a conference call. And after a round of introductions and a little discussion, a man named Craig Grella surfaced as someone who had helped nonprofits to set up help desk software. Craig was a professional at this! He had a whole business that assisted nonprofits and sometimes campaigns in doing this sort of work. He was familiar with several of the help desk products on the market and offered to configure the product and lead the help desk team. Would he have volunteered for any campaign or organization? No, but we weren't any campaign—this was the best way Craig had at that moment to participate in Bernie's political revolution.

Another person on that call was Judie Schumacher, a process engineer who had retired from Wells Fargo, where she had spent a couple of decades overseeing the development of software tools across the organization to help executives teach and reach their goals. I missed her qualifications—because I didn't ask enough specific questions on that first call—but she went to work answering emails on the help desk and would go on to answer several thousand of them. It was only toward the end of the campaign that she finally got into troubleshooting larger process problems that were exposed by the help desk.

Several people came together through a series of trainings that Craig led to form the first iteration of the help desk team. We were so busy with other preparations for July 29th that I spent almost no time on the help desk after that call, save an occasional check-in call with Craig. In those calls he told me about training calls he was holding, videos he was making, and documents he was writing. He created a Frequently Asked Questions document for July 29th, and soon for the campaign in general. Help deskers worked from that document, using canned responses inside the help desk software to answer many questions. The help desk would go on to answer hundreds of thousands of emails over the course of the campaign—and to fight through a backlog of more than one hundred thousand emails that a roomful of paid interns had not been able to put a dent in.

The help desk was the first verification that we could build out a large and powerful central campaign infrastructure using volunteers instead of staff. In fact, it was working so well that we realized, for some functions of a campaign, a team of three or four committed and talented volunteers was equal to or greater than a full-time paid employee. In this case probably greater than, because their combined talents and life experience led to them being able to provide higher quality help desk support than any one person we would have been able to hire to do this task (should we have had the budget to do so). And having a paid staffer replaced by a team of part-time volunteers—instead of a single full-time volunteer—meant that if one volunteer on the team had to drop out, the team could continue on and just recruit a new team member. This is one of the reasons we began to focus on building volunteer teams instead of recruiting individual volunteers to take on discrete tasks on their own.

Our second biggest problem to solve was the map tool that crashed whenever we sent an email out pointing to it. A volunteer software developer named Rapi Castillo had built a beautiful map tool of his own, which posted all of our events on a website that he created. He had whipped it together in a very smart way that new web technology and infrastructure makes possible and even easy. Working with Rapi, I put together a trio of volunteer developers to bring the map into alignment with our site, we moved it over and used it as our official map, and it became a central piece of organizing infrastructure for us that lasted for the rest of the campaign. I believed that the revolution would not be staffed, but I wasn't so sure that could be true about our software development team! To underscore how absolutely key Rapi's contribution was, consider that the second most repeated phrase for Bernie's distributed organizers after "Feel the Bern" was probably "map.berniesanders.com."

The snowball kept growing, building upon itself. A couple of days before July 29th, I created another team—led by Judie Schumacher, who I trusted from her work on the help desk, and Emma Opitz, a recent college grad in western Massachusetts—to curate all the pictures being sent in from events so that we could have a good-looking selection of them for the press and social media.

I'd follow a simple process to form each team:

Step 1: Email a list of between one hundred and one thousand individuals selected as candidates for the team, inviting them to join a conference call. This list could be a random selection of our list, in which case I'd have to email one thousand, or it could be a list based on criteria from the database designed to target people more likely to succeed on the team.

Step 2: Conduct a conference call with the between ten and fifty prospective team members who typically signed up to join. I'd explain the team's purpose, the type of work it would involve, and also the big picture of how we were running a volunteer-driven campaign that would depend on volunteer teams to function.

Step 3: If possible, give the volunteers a task to do to make it onto the team. This would weed out people who, despite the best of intentions, were not serious about doing the work. Sometimes in the beginning, however, I was too busy to set people up with a task and evaluate all the results, so I just let people get started based on a promise that they really wanted to work.

Step 4: Invite a subset of people from the original call who seem to really want to do the work—either because they did the task or promised to—onto another call. On the second call, choose a leader (or two or three coleaders), cover more details about how to get started, and answer questions.

Step 5: Invite the team to a Slack channel or in some other way get them together so that they can productively communicate.

Step 6: Pray they will make it!

The crucial thing to remember in forming volunteer teams is that you don't ask who wants to lead. You ask who wants to get to work. Too often, people think leadership means being a spokesperson or, worse, telling other people what to do without doing any work themselves. It's often hard to judge who will make the best leader in a particular situation or campaign, especially when you are part of a heterogenous movement with lots of talented people ready, willing, and able to get involved. So the best test of leadership is not whether someone self-identifies as a leader. But whether someone is willing and able to do the work, follows through on important tasks, and is willing to be held accountable.

And to be clear: It would have been better to be more deliberate about team building. The Obama folks had the luxury of doing all kinds of team-building activities that really helped teams to function well and be happier. It would have been great if we had had the time to do all that! But we didn't have time, and so we settled for just getting to know each other by working together as peers toward the goal we all shared.

For us, in the chaos of the early campaign, it was all a huge mess. But the snowball kept growing, and more and more work was getting done every day.

I think this part of the story is particularly important for groups that are looking for a way to breathe new life into their work. Any group can build a snowball. We did it without resources and by only accessing a tiny portion of our list. You don't need a presidential candidate. What you need is an urgent cause that people are passionate about. If you have a list of one hundred people who support your cause (and probably you have many more than that), you can invite them onto a conference call. Ten or twenty will show up. Put them to work on a team or two. Throw them into Slack and appoint coleaders. You just quadrupled your organization's capacity!

On July 27th, however, just two days before the kickoff events, Jeff Weaver received an email from a volunteer host asking for help. The email the volunteer host sent included the response he'd originally received from a help desk volunteer—a response that described a much more loosely organized campaign than anyone intended. Jeff forwarded the email to Kenneth, Claire, me, and several other staffers, saying that he was "very skeptical about any organizing program, the basis of which is folks should do whatever comes to mind."

That evening we were due for a call with Jeff to review the plans for July 29th. This was a pretty terrifying time for everyone. The campaign had received very little press so far, and no bad press at all. If the event faced major hiccups, it would be the excuse the mainstream media and establishment Democrats were looking for to point at us and laugh.

This first little conflict with volunteers taking on serious work for the campaign didn't dishearten Kenneth, however, who was encouraged by the incredible amount of work the volunteer teams had done in scarcely more than a week. He explained that volunteers had helped us respond to more than five thousand questions and that 95 percent of those questions were simple to answer—just logistics for the events.

On the call, Jeff was taken aback by the huge numbers of events and RSVPs we were reporting. We were getting close to the final numbers, which would be 2,700 events and one hundred thousand RSVPs—which made it the largest political distributed event ever. It was even bigger than President Obama's biggest general election events in 2012.

Then Bernie joined the call! He sounded astonished by the scale of what was happening. A great many donations had poured in, and a lot of people had turned out to his rallies, but this was the first sign that people were willing to work on their own on a truly unprecedented scale.

Nevertheless, we all remained nervous about the July 29th kick-off events: What if no one showed up? What if something horrible happened at one of the events? A consultant sent a few panicked emails about how each one of the event hosts needed to be officially vetted. Thankfully he was ignored, since there was no capacity to vet 2,700 events. What if the livestream broke? I had fought like crazy to make sure there was a backup internet connection on site, and Jeff had thankfully agreed at the last minute to the expense. Otherwise, we were just depending on some slow cable broadband being shared by a huge apartment building.

In the end, everything went off perfectly with one exception: the DC apartment Claire and I chose to have the livestream event in had weak air conditioning, and with all the people and lights it turned into an oven. Bernie was sweating like crazy when he spoke to the camera, but he didn't complain. And the heat was made up for by our gracious hosts who made everyone feel wonderful, were great on camera, and cooked an incredible feast for everyone, including the press.

Bernie was awed by the experience of speaking directly, live, to one hundred thousand people gathered at homes in every state. It seemed to drive home to him and the whole campaign how big the movement really was. It also made a big impression on the national media, which covered the event widely and began to take the campaign seriously in a new way.

Through the campaign, so many amazing volunteers stepped up to bring their life skills and experience to play staff-equivalent roles on our team: videographers and graphic designers, social workers and restaurant workers, a director of a big-city human resources department, high school students, New Age healers and gritty retired steelworkers and disabled veterans, software developers, bankers, call center managers and, of course, nurses! We took a leap of faith and trusted the volunteers because we believed that was how the revolution should be built—and because we had no choice: Either we gave our supporters staff-equivalent positions, or we had no distributed campaign.

Of course, there were moments when volunteers let us down—but if you've ever been a manager, you know that paid staff also sometimes let you down. Though there's no way to measure something like this empirically, it sure felt as though volunteers were generally more passionate and driven than any staff could ever be. Most volunteers may not be available all day every day, the way staff on a campaign are—but when they are available, they are working hard, throwing themselves into their task fully.

After the second livestream was over—past midnight to catch the West Coast—Claire and I caught a cab back toward our hotel. Even though it was 1:00 a.m., we were so wired that we had to sit down and process where we were. We were pinching ourselves at this bit of history we had walked into. At the same time, we were terrified about the opportunities we knew we were missing.

Forty-five thousand people signed up to volunteer after Bernie's livestream, which was watched by one hundred thousand people at 2,700 events. And almost no one on the campaign knew we were working for it. The campaign wasn't even officially employing us yet! We had not filled out any paperwork, hadn't been paid, and wouldn't be paid for quite some time. But it didn't matter to Claire and me. We had come for the revolution.

Fighting Racism Must Be at the Core of the Message to Everyone

★ becky ★

If it is not led by people of color and immigrants, if it is doesn't have fighting racism and xenophobia at its core, and if it is not mobilizing white people to lead other whites to choose multiracial solidarity over fear and hate—then it's not a revolution.

In most of the movements I've been a part of, and it was certainly true of the Bernie campaign, dismantling structural racism has not been at the heart of the message to everyone. This is a problem, and it's killing people.

It's part of the reason why in July of 2015, in the run-up to the launch of the July 29th kick off events, a group of Black Lives Matter protesters interrupted a candidate town hall at the annual Netroots Nation political conference. Two of the three Democratic candidates for president were on stage—Bernie Sanders and Martin O'Malley. Hillary Clinton, perhaps wanting to avoid likely protests, elected not to attend.

O'Malley's offensive reply came first: "Black lives matter. White lives matter. All lives matter." It's worth noting that Clinton had just a month before provoked a backlash by suggesting "All lives matter" when addressing an audience at an African American church in

Missouri. Bernie followed O'Malley on stage and his response to protesters was to declare, "Black lives, of course, matter. I spent fifty years of my life fighting for civil rights and for dignity." Then he continued "But if you don't want me to be here, that's OK. I don't want to outscream people."

It was in this way that Bernie missed a crucial early opportunity to put race at the center of the message to everyone. It was a failure that continued to damage his ability to bring everyone together around a radical agenda for America, despite what would become the campaign's success at attracting amazing and high-profile surrogates from communities of color. And despite having his first two congressional endorsements come from Congressmen Raul Grijalva and Keith Ellison, the Latino and African American cochairs of the Congressional Progressive Caucus.

It is in this context that we address this rule primarily to white people, though we hope everybody will read it.

We need to listen to the black activists and intellectuals who used the Bernie movement as a teachable moment to explain how another world is possible. They showed us how we can make fighting racism part of our core message to everyone—not just an afterthought aimed at capturing a certain constituency or a profession of personal beliefs or individual acts of solidarity.

Despite the campaign's failures, these black leaders have reached out personally and in the media with patience and love. Their message: The only way to bring down the elites who use race to divide us is to put race at the heart of our fight to build a truly just society. It's time to build a movement that is big enough to win and allows everyone to bring their full selves to the fight.

Consider these statistics. According to Michelle Alexander in her book *The New Jim Crow*, black people are ten times more likely than white people to go to jail for drug use, even though they use drugs at similar rates. And more black people are in prison or the probation/parole system than were enslaved in the 1850s. The Institute for Policy Studies and the Corporation for Enterprise Development published a report, "The Ever-Growing Gap: Failing to Address the Status Quo Will Drive the Racial Wealth Divide for Centuries to

Come," showing that at the current rate the wealth gap is closing, it would take the average black family 228 years to achieve parity with the wealth that white families enjoy today. The richest four hundred Americans have the same amount of wealth as all black people in the United States plus one-third of all Latinos!

Black lives matter. But in the United States, black lives are not valued equally to white lives. Not in the streets, not in the courts, not in our work places, not in our halls of government, not in our schools, not even in our progressive movements for change.

Making change requires more from white people than simply saying "black lives matter" (though that's an important start).

Alicia Garza, a founder of the Black Lives Matter movement, suggested a way forward. Writing in *The Nation* on what's next for the movement that almost elected Bernie Sanders to the White House, she called for our political revolution to "authentically engage and be led by people of color and immigrants" and to hold the Democratic Party accountable for its "epic failure to address the needs of the majority of people in this country." She also asked that white progressives take on the work of "engaging white working-class voters who have been abandoned by the Democrats and exploited by the Republicans."

On the Bernie campaign, immigrants and working class people of color led inspiring, hard-working, and successful campaigns to win votes in their communities. But the leadership of the campaign at the national level—including us—mostly failed to rise to Garza's call to "authentically engage and be led by people of color and immigrants." While we did work to hold the Democratic establishment accountable for abandoning the majority of Americans, Bernie and many of his surrogates primarily spoke to this through the lens of class without adequately addressing race. We did begin to take responsibility for engaging white working class voters. But the rise of Trumpism shows there is still much more work to be done.

We also need to heed the important insights shared by Ian Haney-López and Heather McGhee who, writing specifically about the Bernie Sanders presidential candidacy for *The Nation*, explained that racism is not only crushing black people, but that it is also "a political weapon wielded by elites against the 99 percent, nonwhite and white alike."

Breaking it down further, they explained how "in the post-war era, racism helped create the white middle class. Since the Reagan era, racism has helped destroy it."

In the postwar era, as incomes for whites skyrocketed, elites had a compelling argument to sell white people on maintaining a racist status quo. But since the Reagan era, maintaining the status quo has meant shoring up the plutocratic class even as the white middle and working class see their standards of living eroding. Elites are now using racism and white supremacy to keep struggling whites in line with the elites, no matter that it is not in their economic interest. In this new economic reality, there are openings to organize whites—as Garza also calls us to do—to join a multiracial movement with a vision for an economy that truly works for everybody.

The problem we have to solve is not just that not enough white people believe that black lives matter. It's that not enough white people who say black lives matter are taking action to help dismantle racist structures. White people need to understand that supporting black liberation in a material way is an essential part of any political revolution. We also need to understand that white supremacy is at the heart of the problem—not just a racially associated economic inequality. Our fears of blackness and a white culture that criminalizes blackness are helping to maintain a status quo that benefits the elites to the detriment of working people of all races. Without truly multiracial solidarity, we simply won't be able to build a political revolution big enough to win real change in the United States.

Looking at the Bernie campaign's highest circle of management and influence, it's pretty clear to see that we failed to establish the multiracial leadership that would have been necessary to unite the 99 percent against the billionaire-backed candidates.

I could tell you about specific instances where the campaign fell short in practicing active solidarity with the movement to defend black lives and sometimes got things very wrong. I could also tell you stories of amazing organizing done by Bernie's black, Latino, Muslim, and Native American volunteer leaders who got things exactly right. But I think it suffices to say that we fell short of what the moment required and so missed out on achieving what the moment put within our reach.

How do we go forward?

It's true that climate change, income inequality, war, and Wall Street deregulation disproportionately hurt people of color. But talking about these issues doesn't give white people a pass on addressing race directly.

Yes, Bernie marched with Martin Luther King, Jr., got arrested protesting segregated housing, and was one of the lone white voices in Congress who endorsed and delivered his state to Jesse Jackson's presidential campaign in 1988. Those are personal acts of solidarity, but they do not excuse us from the need to anchor our political analysis in a critique of structural racism.

To change the system—and that's what revolutions aim to do—our movement needs to heed the words of leaders like Garza, Haney-López, and McGhee.

We all must unite to defend black lives and build a movement with authentic leadership from working class people of color and immigrants. We have to hold our parties and our government accountable to the majority of the American people—not corporations, not the 1 percent, and not even just demographics who have historically higher voter turnout. And white people have a special responsibility to ensure that white working and middle class voters choose multiracial solidarity as the only true path to addressing income inequality.

If we don't listen to black leaders and do all these things, our revolution is doomed to fail. The literal war on black people will go on, with the body count going up every day. Participation in a racist system will also continue to hurt white people as they prop up the elites and billionaires who use dog whistle racism to divide the working class. Starting now, we all must unite to defend black lives, or the billionaires win.

Get on the Phone!

★ zack ★

E ven in our digitally connected culture, talking in real time is still absolutely essential in order to develop deeper relationships, keep up with conditions on the ground, and work out tough decisions. Good organizing requires you to get on the phone every day. Use the latest conference call and online scheduling tools to talk more effectively with more people.

After spending my early weeks with the digital team in Washington, DC, launching the July 29th kickoff events, Jeff Weaver told me I should move to Burlington, so I returned home to the Missouri Ozarks for a few days before the long drive up to Vermont.

Preparing for the trip, I sent emails to everyone who had signed up to volunteer in several cities along my route, inviting them to get together to brainstorm with me about how to structure this crazy campaign: Springfield, Saint Louis, Indianapolis, and Columbus. I was going to be in the car for at least five or six hours a day for the next several days—so I gathered a list of promising volunteers who had been showing up on the radar, so that I could call them, get to know them better, and hopefully find an important role for them.

What made someone show up on my radar? An email like the one I received from a guy named Corbin Trent in Tennessee. Corbin blasted out an email to his growing list of Bernie supporters outlining a set of sophisticated goals and strategies for mobilizing volunteers in their state—and the steps he thought it would take to make that happen. He included a link for a conference call so they could get started and get to work.

Somewhere between my little town in the Ozarks and Springfield, Missouri, I called Corbin and found myself in a conversation with a left-wing character whose East Tennessee drawl was music to my Connecticut-born ears.

He was a man of few words, so it took a while, but I pieced together a bit of his story and a few details about the organizing he was attempting in Tennessee. He had no background in politics whatsoever. He had inherited a small, failing factory from his grandfather—one of the last surviving manufacturers of East Tennessee's once-thriving furniture industry. He was sick and tired of watching his community fall into resignation that there was no way to make a living anymore—and he fought to keep the factory open. All the other factories had laid off their employees over the years as they converted to become resellers for much cheaper Chinese-made products. He secured a loan to buy a huge computerized lathe that would dramatically increase productivity and turnaround time.

"And the irony was that it was made in China, right?" I asked.

"Well, I could have bought that one. But I was too stupid and stubborn for that, so I bought the American-made model that cost about four times as much. In hindsight, I can see that I was going out of business one way or another, but I guess I sped up the process with that 'matter of principle.'"

After the factory experience, he went to culinary school, thinking he'd become a chef. And he did—a really good chef. But being a good chef meant that he found himself usually serving rich people, which he found made him angrier and angrier over time. He realized he couldn't take it anymore one day when a group of businessmen walked away from a half-full $3,000 bottle of wine. He quit and started a food truck, Crazy Good Burgers, which became a hit, but then caught on fire—literally on fire—and burned to the ground. Corbin had no insurance, so he became a digital campaigner and fundraiser using GoFundMe and was able to raise enough money to start over. Right after Bernie announced his campaign, Corbin found a buyer for the business—with its "secret seven-step process recipe for Crazy Good Fries"—and resolved to stretch the earnings as long as possible to volunteer for Bernie full time in Tennessee.

He told me about his attempts to organize Tennessee so far. He was driving all over the place, meeting with local leaders who had surfaced in the July 29th kickoff events.

I talked with Corbin several times on that trip across the country. I probed and confirmed that he had really never done anything political before. I considered whether I might be able to rely on him as a core team leader, which would mean giving him some authority to access sensitive data.

He seemed like such an improbable character—I worried that he was a right-wing prankster who had figured out exactly how to hack our open, volunteer-driven campaign. Was he improbable? Hadn't I been saying for my entire political life that if we asked the people to do something big enough, all kinds of amazing, talented, previously unpolitical—and normal—people would come out of the woodwork in droves? And here they were. Corbin was the first of thousands of stunning, previously nonpolitical volunteers who took leadership in the campaign. Bernie's big ask for the political revolution was bringing them out.

All this happened on the phone. I spent probably three or four hours on the phone with Corbin between my house in the Ozarks and Burlington. I spent all day, every day on the phone, and by the time I got to Vermont, I had the beginnings of a solid core volunteer team.

The only way I could have possibly gotten to know Corbin and the dozen other future leaders I recruited on that trip was by talking to them on the phone. Sure, face to face would have been better, but the Bernie campaign was and the revolution is national in scale—we have to make do with the phone.

When I started out as a union organizer, we spent hours every day doing "call time"—following up with members of our organizing committees. We had to do call time from whatever dingy hotel we were working out of, hunched over our notes on the bed because the phone cord didn't reach to the desk. I remember thinking ahead to a cell phone future and thinking how great it was going to be to do call time from the car on the way home from house visits, or from a café or park! But when the digital organizing future did come, we seemed to put away the phone forever. Instead of organizing committees of dozens, we had membership lists of thousands, or millions. What sense could it make to call only 0.0001 percent of one's membership? What could be accomplished that way?

When the center of the organizing world moved from small community, labor, or campaign organizations to mass "internet organizations" with huge loose memberships, real organization building seemed to disappear—and the few attempts to resurrect it by building old-style chapter organizations from established email lists have ultimately failed despite some valiant efforts. Those failures were determined by many factors, but one of them was the resistance that "online organizers" had to embrace the old-fashioned daily work of getting on the phone with volunteer leaders—and even with paid organizing staff.

One thing that old-school organizing wisdom has right is that one-on-one personal contact is a required ingredient in organizing. But in the era of small organizing, "one-on-ones" came to be seen as the only path to get supporters to take even the smallest of actions—such as signing a union card or a petition to the city to place a stop sign at a busy neighborhood intersection. The big organizing framework rejects that as a rock-piling approach to organizing. A few weeks into Bernie's campaign, tens of thousands of people had already taken the first step of donating and signing up to volunteer. Thousands had come together in person at meetings organized over Facebook. Corbin was already driving around Tennessee buying voter files from counties and having his own one-on-ones with leaders who were already at work organizing their own communities before I had even joined the campaign.

What I was doing with Corbin was just the normal, natural process of getting to know one of my colleagues in the movement, a peer who I would need to work alongside in order to succeed. My free-ranging conversations did not follow a set format—such as the "five steps of a one-on-one" that I had learned as a union organizer—but instead sought to simply get to know him, learn all that I could from him, and develop a truly mutual relationship that would hopefully become the basis of a productive partnership.

In big organizing, we get back to building organizations by empowering thousands of people on our lists to become builders. (The central volunteer Slack for the Bernie campaign was actually called "Bernie Builders.") But you don't start with thousands. You start with dozens—or even just one. And the only way you get those first few leaders engaged, since they almost certainly don't live near you, is to get on the phone.

Getting on the phone is a skill that's mostly missing from the digital organizer's repertoire even as phone technology is being revolutionized by new tools and opportunities in the era of big organizing. Talking on the phone is absolutely essential for identifying, recruiting, and managing volunteer leaders—and for building and nurturing relationships.

Spending a chunk of each day calling volunteers may sound like an inefficient use of staff time. Digital staffers talking to people on the phone? They should be on the computer not on the phone, right? In a big campaign like Bernie 2016, thousands of people were emailing us every day demanding support or telling us about emergencies that we needed to solve in their local campaign worlds. It was very difficult to justify getting on the phone with just a handful of people each day.

But when you've only got a few full-time staffers and you're being bombarded by thousands of unserved volunteers—or worse, you have thousands of inactive people on your list—then you had better start recruiting some new, committed, talented leaders to form an organization that can realize the full potential of your membership. Beyond recruitment, phone calls should be a staple of your daily organization-building work, accomplishing all sorts of different purposes.

You may say, even if I had time to get on the phone, scheduling calls is a nightmare! As someone with time management issues, I'll share here one of my favorite tricks on the Bernie campaign for getting people on the phone with me efficiently: I would email a large group of people to invite them to talk if they were available, with a link to a web-based scheduling tool. On the campaign we used tools like YouCanBook.me or Calendly, but the tool itself isn't important. You just need something to avoid the hassle of back-and-forth messages to schedule a call. Sometimes it's appropriate to get on the phone with people in small batches. A simple low-tech way to do this is to create a Google spreadsheet that anyone can edit, add the time slots you want to fill, and send the link to your people so they can sign up for available time slots.

There are free conference call services that make joining conference calls even easier because they don't require pins to access. For calls with over one hundred participants, you may need a more full-service conference call system—but even monthly subscriptions to these more full-service tools are available at a low cost.

Perhaps the most powerful thing you can do on the phone is to form a new team—and you can do it using one simple conference call. This huge opportunity emerges from the relatively new combination of campaign email lists, cheap conference call tools, and the fact that everyone carries phones with them at all times. Countless times on the Bernie campaign, work teams were launched by sending out an email to a portion of the list with an invitation to a conference call. The invite might have said something along the lines of:

Dear Supporter, We have an important job that needs doing, and we think you could help. If you have time, please join me on a conference call at 2:00 ET at the number below, and I'll tell you all about what we need and answer your questions. If you don't have time today, don't worry—I'll email you another day to get you involved.

As a rule of thumb, if we emailed one hundred people who had signed up to volunteer but were not yet involved, we would wind up with about fifteen to twenty people on the phone—even with just a few hours' notice. Your conversion rates will vary, but the idea is that if you email people, some percentage will actually get on the phone with you! There's no need to overthink the scheduling. There didn't seem to be a lift in giving people more notice. We actually preferred to give people only a few hours' notice because we tended to attract people who were more available that way—people who were unemployed, retired, or for whatever other reason totally available and incredibly eager to work on the campaign.

On the call, we would do a round of introductions, which would allow us to get an initial read on who might be a good, clear-headed leader—and who might lack key interpersonal skills, such as the ability to listen to others. We would then explain the task at hand and find out who was ready and qualified to get to work. Teams like the one managing the help desk all started when I—and some volunteers—picked up the phone.

Beyond forming teams, phone conversations are key for strengthening relationships with individual volunteer leaders and tracking their progress.

For some reason, getting to know volunteers on the phone—or even in person—is not something that comes easily to many organizers. To get someone's story, all you have to do is ask. Everyone wants to tell their story. Simply ask, "What's your story?" But people are so unused to this direct question that you normally have to ask two or three times. What happens when you get to know volunteer leaders like this is that you begin to develop a peer relationship among colleagues.

Regularly checking in with volunteer leaders on the phone also allows you to troubleshoot their work and help them improve in their roles. And there may be some moments in a campaign when you have to call your volunteer leaders to inspire them with the long-term vision that they may not fully understand yet. If you are higher up the chain of command, you probably have a lot more visibility into the coolest parts of the campaign. You can see victories or potential victories coming. Tell your volunteer leaders about them.

Through all these conversations with individual leaders, you will learn what is going on out there in your movement. This is one of the most important reasons to spend time on the phone. If you know what volunteers are facing, if you know what's working and what's not working, then you will be able to make and argue for decisions that are in tune with the reality of the conditions on the ground. If you've spent enough time on the phone with volunteers, and listened carefully to what they have to say, then you won't be one of those organizers who comes up with ideas that'll never fly, or shoots down ideas that could transform the campaign.

The Work Is Distributed.
The Plan Is Centralized.

★ becky ★

In distributed organizing, the work may be distributed, but if you're going to win something big, you need a centralized plan. Instead of letting a thousand flowers bloom, build a networked flower factory. Delegate chunks of work from a centralized, strategic campaign plan to a distributed network of volunteer leaders who can work across space and time, and in the numbers necessary, to meet concrete goals that put victory within reach.

The unlikely success of the Bernie campaign was powered in part by distributed organizing. Two million eight hundred thousand people donated money. Hundreds of thousands of people volunteered their time. The vast majority of these supporters never saw the inside of a field office. While the other campaign had big-dollar contributors and all of the resources that the establishment could muster, we had people. Lots of them.

By the time the Iowa caucus rolled around, it was clear to the whole nation that there was a massive and passionate movement answering Bernie Sanders's call to build a political revolution. But for people who were early supporters of the campaign or who follow organizing with interest (and that describes me on both counts), it was six months earlier that we saw the first indications that the political revolution Bernie called for in his stump speech might actually happen. That was when over 2,700 Bernie supporters responded to emails from the campaign and held house parties attended by over one hundred thousand people and watched Bernie talk about his revolution on a livestream webcast.

This was an astounding feat for any politician, much less a shouty seventy-four-year-old Jewish Democratic socialist from Vermont, who most people thought of at the time as an insignificant protest candidate for president. In the wake of those July 29th grassroots campaign events, many Bernie supporters—including me—realized that if enough of us got involved, we might actually win this thing.

This is what Zack and I were discussing in a flurry of phone calls back in August of 2015, when I was still running politics and philanthropy at CREDO Mobile. He was calling me, sometimes daily, to talk about how to solve the organizing challenges, big and small, that he and Claire were facing now that they had launched this crazy distributed organizing program that was getting big fast.

Zack is a brilliant organizer who thinks deeply about the mechanics of movements. At this point in the campaign he was obsessed with increasing volunteer capacity, and particularly with putting the transformation of supporters into local volunteer team leaders on a sustainable and measurable growth path. In the beginning, he was using the crude measure of week-over-week growth of events on map.berniesanders.com to see if the model was working. Everything on the distributed team was being managed to produce more event hosts, more events posted, more RSVPs. The kinds of questions he was asking were "How do we get more volunteers to become leaders?" and "How do we get one-time event hosts to make their events recurring?"

This was typical of our interactions throughout a decade and a half of working in the movement together. I was amazed at what Zack was doing, but I had a question. To which Zack replied, "Oh, right (long pause). How do we do that?"

The question was pretty simple. "When are you going to get these people calling voters? Because what you have them doing now doesn't help win elections."

As I talked to Zack while walking circles around my block in San Francisco, our discussions kept looping back to the same topic. Zack stayed focused on growing capacity, and I was becoming increasingly worried about the fact that flyering at farmers markets or standing at busy intersections waving signs at cars does not impact the outcome of elections.

Even when volunteers did focus on contacting voters (entirely of their own accord, not at the direction of the campaign), they were setting up canvasses that would never be able to return data to the campaign's main voter file. People were developing software, building websites, writing music. They wanted to do something, anything to help Bernie. In the absence of clear instructions from Burlington to supporters in states that had no staff, volunteers just started making stuff up. Much of it was glorious, some of it was crazy, but we knew it was far, far less than the sum of its parts. It was like presidential campaigning as a game of exquisite corpse.

"Growth is great, but it's not going to help you win if you don't get these people doing voter contact in geographies that matter," I kept drilling into Zack's head.

At that point in the campaign, thousands of people outside the four states that would vote first were essentially running their own mini campaigns with their singularly home-brewed strategies. To make matters worse, the largest concentration of volunteers was in California, my home state. It was both awesome and upsetting because I knew that without the ability for all these people to contribute to a central campaign plan, Bernie could be out of the race before Californians ever got to cast a ballot in a June primary that was nearly a year away.

"Look, the Obama campaign taught Californians that the way we can help a candidate win a presidential campaign is to talk to people in Nevada. You have to get them off the street corners doing honk and waves and into phone banks where they can start piling up volunteer voter contacts where it really matters," I offered as a solution.

"Start setting up phone banks so volunteers can talk to voters. You can make it massive. That's how you can help win the election."

As a veteran of two presidential campaigns, I knew Zack hated the fact that the volunteer asks he and Claire were making were so vague and unconnected to a field plan. It was exasperating to even consider that the campaign might get huge but still be doomed. In those early days of the campaign, they had no access to the campaign's voter file outside of the first four states, and they certainly didn't have staff on the ground. They were also constantly exhausted. For the first few months it was just the two of them doing the organizing in the forty-six states that were not Iowa, New Hampshire, Nevada, and South Carolina.

While I didn't know Claire as well, I knew she shared Zack's revolutionary orientation. I admired the organizing she'd done going up against the establishment and eventually winning when she cofounded Frack Action in New York State. There she took on not only the fossil fuel companies but also the more established environmental groups to win a moratorium on fracking that few thought possible.

Zack and Claire were not electoral field organizers. Neither one of them had even ever sat down and called voters as part of a phone bank. Organizing volunteer voter contact is something I'd done in 2012 and 2014. It wasn't rocket science, but it was a lot of hard work. I had run operations that did over one million volunteer phone calls to voters. But the potential for Bernie was bigger than anything I'd thought possible.

So finally one day in late August, I told Zack: "If you can get me hired on to your team, I'll quit my job and join the campaign. We'll figure out how to turn this crazy growth machine into something that makes a contribution to the national field plan and can help Bernie win."

It's important to acknowledge that it can feel counterintuitive to use the word "centralized" in reference to our distributed organizing.

In the world of digital organizing, the idea of centralization, with the exception of fundraising, was increasingly becoming anathema. What we did on the Bernie campaign was the opposite of strategies we'd seen employed by digital giants like Change.org, who invest a significant amount of organizing capital in offering tools to individual activists and encouraging them to run millions of small and independent campaigns, mostly via petition.

Those campaigns primarily work as multipliers. For example, in addition to having ten rallies organized by a national nonprofit's staff in major cities, if you added a distributed element, you'd have one hundred rallies because activists would be allowed to create their own events. Or say a group is running a campaign targeting five major newspapers with an ask to stop referring to undocumented immigrants as "illegals." A distributed strategy would ask members to run the same campaign targeting their smaller local news outlets.

On the Bernie campaign, we didn't need to multiply the activities of the national staff. We needed to take one huge task—actually building a massive voter contact machine—and break it up into little chunks that volunteers could start knocking out on a day-by-day basis. As celebrated as the "distributed" aspects of the volunteer organizing behind the Bernie campaign have been, all this work would not have had the same impact had the work not also been part of a highly centralized plan.

So while we knew we needed to contact millions of voters in every state, we also knew we needed to contact them in an order that had the biggest impact on winning the state primaries and caucuses, each with its own set of rules and deadlines for registration, vote-by-mail process, in-person voting, and caucus participation. We also needed help running the national technology and local organizing infrastructure necessary to pull this all off.

As longtime progressive organizers and witnesses to more drum circles than we care to acknowledge, both Zack and I respected our movement's affinity for decentralization. I remember an excited conversation we had as we got into a rental car at the Denver International Airport in my early days on the campaign. Zack and I were on our way to a barnstorm meeting in Colorado Springs where over 150 activists in the heart of conservative Colorado were waiting for us to arrive and tell them how they could help Bernie win their state. As we were throwing our bags in the back of the rental, we talked explicitly about what the digital organizing department was going to have to do. How could we escape the default attitude of "let a thousand flowers bloom" (a common misquotation of the Maoist slogan "let one hundred flowers bloom") that dominated the thinking of so many digital campaigners and volunteers? And yet, there was something about "let a thousand flowers bloom" that was important to keep. Zack put his finger on it when he said, "But really we need to create a giant, nationwide distributed flower factory!" We laughed and then agreed that this was a campaign story we should never tell!

But before I could truly get my hands dirty and join Zack in this work of building a distributed structure to help volunteers to the voter contact work of a centralized campaign plan, I had to get hired! It wasn't until several weeks after I agreed to come on board that I was summoned to Burlington in September 2015 to interview with Bernie's close advisor Phil Fiermonte.

In Phil's office, I pitched my qualifications for joining the distributed organizing team, while Zack and Claire sat nervously on the couch hoping this somehow wasn't about to fall through. Like the hundreds of thousands of volunteers who would be activated across the country, I shared Bernie's political analysis and that was why I was willing to quit my job and go all in to elect him president.

I explained to Phil that I wanted to draw on my digital and field experience at CREDO SuperPAC to help channel all of the volunteer energy from the Bernie grassroots into accomplishing work that was laid out in the national field plan. The volunteer organizing was on pace to match the campaign's record-breaking fundraising. But if the work that volunteers were given didn't advance the campaign's field strategy—with specific goals and targets for having conversations with voters in key states—we'd successfully organize a lot of people but we wouldn't be doing anything at scale to help Bernie win.

It must have gone okay. Ten days later I was in Washington, DC, where I was attending a legal meeting for digital rights groups who were intervening on behalf of the FCC to defend net neutrality rules from a court challenge launched by big telecom. That's when I got the call from Phil. I was on board what was then called the digital organizing team and incredibly grateful that Phil had given me the opportunity.

Once I was in, I found myself in a position I had always tried to avoid in my career. At this point in the campaign, Zack, Claire, and I were pretty much 100 percent overhead. If voter contact and donations are how you produce marginal value in a campaign, we were producing no value.

The one hundred thousand people who attended the 2,700 house parties to watch Bernie on the livestream talk about how to get involved in the campaign amounted to a magnificent distributed organizing accomplishment. But it wasn't yet clear how it contributed to the plan to help Bernie win. We had to get the volunteers recruited at those events to start producing value for the campaign by knocking out voter contacts as part of the campaign's national field plan.

The first step was to get the volunteers making calls to voters in distributed phone banks into the key early states we absolutely had to win. The problem was, the field program hadn't asked the distributed team to work on this, which meant they weren't assigning us goals, and they weren't giving us numbers of voters to call.

We believed we could create a capacity to make millions of calls. And we desperately wanted to contribute to the national field plan in a substantial, measurable, and accountable way. But no one had ever done this at scale in a primary before, so we didn't blame the field program for not writing our volunteers into substantial roles in state plans. For all they knew, our plan was complete bunk.

Soon after I was hired, Rich Pelletier was named national field director and started hiring state staff for the Super Tuesday states. Rich was a progressive strategist who had helped move money and resources into federal races as the field director at America Votes. He was thoughtful, cared about the states, and demonstrated a real interest in the potential to turn the energies of all our out-of-state volunteers into a virtual voter contact machine.

That said, Rich faced huge challenges. Hiring professionals to work for an unconventional candidate in the 2016 presidential cycle was brutal; even though Bernie had proved that he could raise the money to compete, it was hard for the campaign to hire experienced field people. In the early days of the campaign, before our stupendous successes would become evident, there was a real fear out there for people who made their careers in DC that they could be blackballed by the Democratic establishment for joining the Bernie campaign. And the campaign was cautious with precious financial resources and, so, was slow to approve even the smallest and most mundane program decisions if money was involved. Rich had many fires to put out before he would ever be able to put serious thought into a crazy scheme like ours.

We sincerely appreciated his support amid the chaos that tends to define insurgent presidential campaigns, and we plunged forward continuing to build volunteer capacity. As soon as Rich and his field department were ready for us to spring into action, we wanted to be able to point our firehose of tens of thousands (and later it would be over one hundred thousand) of volunteers at whatever targets they gave us.

To be honest, I was deeply concerned that at some point someone on the campaign was going to look at the budget of the distributed organizing department and then divide it by the number of voter contacts we had logged in VAN and that the numerator was going to be too big and the denominator was going to be zero.

Then the campaign could—and should!—pull the plug on the whole big crazy rare wonderful magic thing that was happening with the volunteers out in the forty-six states. We had to get our people doing voter contact ASAP, and for volunteers all across the country, that meant getting on the phone and calling voters in the four staffed states where people could vote for Bernie in February.

But the reality we faced in the fall of 2015 was that neither the Bernie campaign nor the Clinton campaign was building the kind of capacity we saw was possible in the later states. The national field operation was focused on the first four states, Iowa and New Hampshire especially. To many observers' surprise, the campaign was already going toe to toe with the Clinton campaign's operations in those states. And the campaign was just getting started in Nevada and South Carolina.

In the vacuum, the national field team adopted an intense localism, working to support the state operations that were already up and running on the ground. This was standard for presidential campaigns and actually made a lot of sense. There were strong leaders in Iowa and New Hampshire—Robert Becker and Julia Barnes. Both states were run as stand-alone campaigns. This was a model that could work in the early primaries—brilliantly in New Hampshire where we won and in Iowa where we fought to an unlikely virtual tie.

Rich understood the power of using out-of-state volunteers to supercharge local voter outreach efforts, and he encouraged our efforts. If we could have out-of-state phone bankers do all the voter identification calls (figuring out who was for Bernie, who would never vote for Bernie, and who was undecided) it would free up his in-state staff to knock on doors and do persuasion. And since we had scale nationally with volunteer recruitment, we could not only call through the targeted universe but call all the independent voters or even Republicans to identify every last voter who might be for Bernie at no opportunity cost to the local staff and volunteers!

Still, in the chaotic environment of a start-up, insurgent presidential primary campaign, we struggled to get our volunteers incorporated into the field goals of the early states or to ensure that the state data directors allocated us a targeting universe to call.

Our hope was that after the first two states, the national volunteer base would be better integrated into the field strategy. Because of the eccentricities of the US primary calendar, there are particular strategies, tactics, and economics that make sense in the caucus in Iowa and the primary in New Hampshire but are unsustainable as a chain reaction of contests are unleashed following the first few states to cast ballots. There comes a point when you have to "beat the Iowa out of people" as an Obama field veteran explained to us—talking about the moment when Iowa organizers find themselves tasked with organizing a whole country, not just one small state.

The nation's eyes are on those first two contests, and to compete there you hire a relatively huge staff, open a couple dozen offices, and the candidate spends an inordinate amount of time there engaged in retail politicking. It is simply not possible to apply that template as the campaign moves on from focusing on two key contests for months in advance to getting ready for eleven simultaneous primaries and caucuses on Super Tuesday, and then a rapid succession of states voting after that. Eventually, the campaign would need the national volunteers, who were already begging us to put them to work by the thousands, to fill the void and take on the lion's share of voter contact, and a plan to mobilize them effectively to do just that.

By the time I joined we were all firmly focused on the rapidly approaching Iowa and New Hampshire contests because if we didn't outperform expectations there, we would be dead in our tracks and Super Tuesday would be the effective end of the campaign.

I asked the national data team to pull voters from the voter file that weren't being called in-state. They reported back that they took orders from the state data directors. These state staffers were committed to helping Bernie win, but they were also generally pretty junior and highly overworked. Getting their attention was difficult because they were already overwhelmed with operational work and the numbers they had to deliver to their state directors.

Partly as a consequence of focusing on state plans at this point rather than a national field plan, the national data team had to function both as the department that drove smart decisions about data for a presidential campaign and as a service bureau for the local offices, with the latter being prioritized. Since our team was not a traditional state campaign, and not even technically located in the field department, it was difficult to get the data we needed to drive our program.

We were trapped. We knew we needed all the volunteers we were working with in the states outside of the first four primaries to start doing voter contact. But campaigns are hierarchies with strict command and control. So we continued to build volunteer capacity by trying to grow the number of people holding events such as debate watch parties for the October and November debates.

It all came to a head in October. Every morning at 10:30 a.m., the digital team gathered on a conference call to discuss the email calendar and other relevant happenings. This included digital fundraising, social media, organizing, and the state digital directors in the first four early voting states. On the agenda was an email series inviting supporters to another big round of distributed events that were not focused on voter contact.

Michael Whitney at Revolution Messaging was running over the email calendar section of meeting that Tim Tagaris ran with the brutal efficiency of the Marine that he once was. Michael barked at us about recruiting hosts for upcoming debate watch parties. How was watching debates going to help us win the election and shouldn't we be making the pivot to voter contact at this point?

Argh! It was crazy-making to have a much younger digital fundraising consultant tell me something I already knew about our organizing program. But I wasn't going to make excuses, because on a presidential campaign, if you can't win support for your plans, that's on you. The answer was simply, "Yes, you're right. That's exactly what we need to do."

Then we had a breakthrough. We heard about a super volunteer in California named Ceci Hall. Somehow, she had gotten in touch with one of our Iowa field organizers. The organizer, Nate Rifkin, was quietly running a ring of out-of-state Bernie phone bankers in California by doling out access codes to the phone bank software for getting Iowa volunteers to make calls. This was what the distributed team should be doing but at a huge, huge scale. Not only was Ceci making calls to voters on a daily basis, she was traveling around Southern California recruiting and training other volunteers to do the same thing.

We wanted to know how a random volunteer in Orange County, one of the most conservative corners of Southern California, had gotten ahead of the distributed organizers who were actually on staff.

As it turns out, Ceci's success wasn't random at all, but it's also important to note that she was the kind of person who never would have made it to the interview stage if the so-called political professionals on the team (like me) had listed a job for an organizer to join our team to recruit and train a network of remote phone bank hosts. In retrospect, she had a near-perfect resume.

Ceci had never been an organizer or even an activist. But she had a deep understanding of the power of talking to people on the phone. She was a former broker, having sold financial services for nearly two decades, much of that time with Washington Mutual, a savings and loan that catered to working class and middle class consumers.

She'd moved up through the ranks and ended up managing teams of virtual financial advisors working out of call centers. WaMu went down in the 2007–2008 financial meltdown, but when JPMorgan Chase took the bank over in 2008, they kept Ceci on. At Chase, Ceci ended up training the offshore staff in countries like the Philippines that the bank was using to replace the workers still on its own payroll in US-based call centers. Eventually, in the spring of 2015, it was finally Ceci's turn to get laid off. Coincidentally this was exactly at the same time that Bernie Sanders launched his candidacy for the Democratic presidential nomination.

People like Ceci who saw the financial meltdown from the inside (and also from the downside) often get what's going on in this country on a more personal level than people who work in seemingly recession-proof industries like the nonprofit sector or political consulting. Coming out of the crash, she was aware of news reports that the economy was growing, but things weren't getting better under Barack Obama for the people in her own life. She also had two younger sisters with advanced degrees, who were drowning in student debt and struggling to find jobs. In her own words, she came to realize that "anybody born in the 90s is screwed" and their standard of living was, for the first time in generations, going to go down not up. But this guy Bernie Sanders was speaking to the issues she cared about—the country needed to stop bailing out the big banks and start looking out for regular people like her.

Ceci tried to plug in to her local Bernie groups, but they were organizing events like "honk and waves" that she thought were a waste of time. What's more, she was sick of some of the groups' leadership "telling her what she could and couldn't do." So she started hunting for an actual Bernie staffer. Ceci and a like-minded friend hit the phones and started asking everyone they could find who was volunteering for Bernie if they knew anyone who was actually on the staff of the Bernie campaign.

The two of them eventually connected with a San Diego State student who was phone banking into Iowa as part of a college group organized by Iowa field staffer Nate Rifkin. Ceci convinced Nate to put her on an email distribution list for the college student activists he was organizing, and it was through that network that she gained access to the codes that unlocked the virtual phone banks targeting Iowa voters.

Not only did Ceci begin phone banking but she recruited others to join her, starting with Orange County, then expanding to Glendale, and finally reaching out to people in Northern California where she connected with a Democratic Party activist in Sacramento named Eric Sunderland. Eric was also running phone banks into Iowa via Nate, and they decided to team up and pull in San Francisco for Bernie by offering technical support and some training help.

When we started digging into it, we discovered there were other field organizers running groups of out-of-state volunteers just like they ran their in-state volunteers: connecting with them one-on-one, giving them voter contact tasks, and checking in with them along the way. It was good old-school organizing but it was labor intensive, extremely decentralized, and a small-organizing approach when compared to what a big distributed organizing approach could unleash.

We hired Ceci into one of the rare hiring slots that were added for the national distributed organizing team. Her mission would be to leverage the campaign's massive email list to recruit tens of thousands of people to do the work that she already had hundreds of fellow supporters in California engaged in. We were ready to start building the voter contact machine, and it was going to be people like Ceci who were going to make it happen.

That's how it began. We simply made our own goals and picked the targets that seemed best in line with the campaign's overall strategy, but we were always ready to move the firehose in whatever direction field asked when they discovered additional capacity was needed in a crucial contest. But we had another problem. We actually had to convince our newly thrown together army of volunteer leaders, who were for the most part antiauthoritarian, anticorporate, intersectional feminist populists, to do what we asked them and get on the phone!

Throughout the campaign, we accomplished a huge amount of work through independent organizing that happened outside of staffed field offices. Eventually "the Bernie dialer," as we called our centralized calling program, had the capacity to call every single voter in key states like Nevada nearly on a daily basis. Of course, most people wouldn't have picked up but a lot would. Traditionally campaigns call only likely voters they think might be on their side. What if we had thrown out the conventional wisdom and simply called everyone? It could have been game changing. We developed the capacity to do this, but we never pulled the trigger on it. Instead of thinking of that as a missed opportunity, we believe it represents a great hope for the future. A public interest campaign for an audacious policy goal or another insurgent candidate can tap into this capacity in the grassroots and start approaching civic engagement in a radically bigger and potentially far more powerful way than most campaigns are run today.

What made this even more of a break with the current orthodoxies that insist your campaign can only be as big as you have money to pay people was that this work was accomplished in large part by volunteers managed by other volunteers—no other presidential primary in recent history had done this. Volunteers weren't only asked to call voters, they were also asked to run huge parts of the campaign's digital organizing technology infrastructure, including our virtual call center and our peer-to-peer texting program. Some of them even opened rogue volunteer offices!

Not all movements have such clear objectives and deadlines as electing a candidate to office—where your goal is to identify, persuade, and turnout more voters than your opponent, with Election Day as the ultimate deadline. Not all campaigns have a clear leader at the top—the candidate—who will be able to say "this is how we win and we need everyone who supports me to get in line with our strategy."

It's important to recognize that a revolution won't be launched by consensus. As organizers or volunteer leaders, you need to propose a strategic plan and invite others to join you. Don't worry about being undemocratic. If your plan is not smart enough, not enough people will join you, and you can give up on the revolution and become a small nonprofit instead!

Any group of changemakers—from a small affinity group to a large organization to a revolutionary movement with clear demands—can benefit from adopting this rule. Create a centralized strategic plan using whatever process is right for your movement. Make sure the plan has tasks that can be repeated by volunteers that add up to progress on the plan. Then delegate chunks of work from your plan to a distributed network of volunteer leaders who can work across space and time, and in the numbers necessary, to meet concrete goals and make change possible.

The Revolution Will Be Funded—by Small Donations

★ zack ★

I f you spend your time and energy asking rich people to support your movement, then your movement isn't going to get anywhere. Spend your time talking to the people you are trying to organize, building your movement and resources as they are needed will come. Do not become part of the nonprofit industrial complex by claiming to be helping people who care about you so little that they won't pitch in a few bucks to support your work.

The Bernie campaign raised over $231 million from 2.8 million individual donors. Bernie didn't have to spend time talking to big-dollar donors or flying to California to go to fundraisers. He was blissfully free to be talking to voters in upcoming states through the whole campaign.

On the fundraising side, Tim Tagaris and his team at Revolution Messaging, working with Kenneth Pennington, who was the digital staffer that Bernie trusted to pull this all off, were doing something radical. They were telling the truth. There was no subject line from Bernie reading all lowercase "hey." No one was going to win dinner with Bernie Sanders, much less George Clooney. It wasn't even that they tested those gimmicks and found they didn't payoff. It was always about delivering Bernie's message, treating the people on the other side of the email as smart people who were our peers not someone to be fleeced by the latest marketing tactic. It was about being honest. The messages were that Bernie was a long shot, and moneyed interests might be too powerful to overcome. That what we were talking about was nothing less than a political revolution and it would only work if millions of people joined us. That the middle class will surely collapse if we didn't change course right now.

As a result, the email team was killing it nearly every single day. Michael Whitney was as spectacular an email writer as Tim. And they both shared a deep and abiding animosity toward the corporate and political establishment players that were pulling out all the stops to take Bernie down. Tim had run digital operations for Ned Lamont's stunning Senate primary upset of Joe Lieberman in 2006 (only to be defeated when Lieberman ran in the general as an Independent, capturing plenty of Republican voters). Michael had made a name for himself on the left running campaigns for the radical left-flank political blog, *Firedoglake*. *Firedoglake* coined the term "veal pen" in 2009 to describe how the Obama administration had stitched up liberal groups and rendered them toothless on Democratic accountability in his first term.

Raising small-dollar contributions so Bernie could go up against the establishment and win wasn't just a job for Michael and Tim. It was their life mission! So much so that on October 1, 2015, when Bernie was still flying coach, the campaign announced that it had raised $26 million in the period since July. It was an astonishing number. To put it in context, it was more than President Obama had raised during the same period in 2007 when he was at the beginning of his improbable but eventually successful primary campaign against Hillary Clinton. The major media reported it, and it was one of the first signs to the outside world that something amazing and unprecedented was happening with the Bernie campaign. I've been doing email fundraising since the medium was invented, and I can say with certainty that Tim's team was the best I've seen in the history of this business.

We knew in late September that Bernie's political revolution was definitely going to be funded—with small-dollar contributions from supporters.

Bernie's small-dollar funding base was far from a given. But we did know that Bernie was not going to participate in the pay-to-play system that leaves even the most progressive campaigns beholden to rich people who can put up the money for day-to-day expenses.

In 2007, the national activist organization of radical feminists of color, Incite, published a long-overdue manifesto called *The Revolution Will Not be Funded*. The cover is a photograph of men in suits feasting on a rich buffet at some donor conference, with name tags identifying their organizations. The authors argue that organizations will be afraid to consider radical directions if they are dependent upon funding by the nonprofit industrial complex.

I have seen the problem of foundation funding from another angle. Several times, I've watched major donors and activists attempt to collaborate to start up a "revolutionary" campaign around a pressing issue of our time. Each time, the effort was doomed even before the official launch.

One of these times I witnessed close up across a couple of climate change summits held at the former family estate of an actual nineteenth century oil baron. A bunch of big shots of the nonprofit world and a handful of young organizers wined and dined for three days straight. We went for walks in the woods and were treated to a tour of the estate, complete with family stories of the founding patriarch. A big-time corporate branding agency was hired to come up with just the right name and logo for the campaign this group had been assembled to launch. A couple of digital agencies were hired to create the website, write mass emails, and guide the online campaign. Top field organizers were hired to build a nationwide organizing team. Tens of millions of dollars were pledged—and the money was in fact spent.

But then, almost nothing happened. What was the problem? The name and logo were smart and beautiful. The digital agencies were brilliant. The field organizers were the best in the business. Scores of celebrity endorsers were lined up. So why didn't a brand-new and powerful climate movement spring up and change everything?

Here's the fundamental problem with trying to launch the revolution on foundation money: The stewards of all those foundation billions are not going to pay you to overthrow the system. The people running the nonprofits participating in the coalition are not going to support you when you try to blow everything up. They can't because they are dependent on that money—and money almost always comes with at least one string attached: the one that says you can't blow everything up.

When it comes to climate change—as Naomi Klein brilliantly documented in her book *This Changes Everything*—some of the largest environmental groups and their supporting industry of consultants are deeply in the pockets of big corporations and their charitable arms. The plans they propose simply don't call for change as fast as we need it. And in this case, gradual change means catastrophe.

At the robber baron summit for creating a new group to fight climate change, the donors didn't come right out and tell the campaigners to set their sights low. They didn't have to. Everyone who was invited knew that truly radical climate solutions were not on the table.

Another, simpler way to say all this is: No revolution has ever been launched with paid mercenaries and a branding agency. Ever. And it never will be.

I definitely don't blame anyone for trying. I went to those summits after all! I drank their good wine and gave my two cents along with everyone else. With all the newness of the internet era, it made sense to see if there was a new way to launch world-changing projects online. But after almost twenty years of internet-powered politics, I think we can call it: If you want to overthrow the system, or any part of it, you still need to start with the people.

Okay. Fine. But then where will the money come from?

First of all, what Becky and I are saying is that revolutions usually are begun with no central source of funding. Start with people, not with money. The rest of this is largely devoted to how that can be done.

But as you grow your base among the people, the great thing about the internet era is that you can also raise money on the internet in small donations from the same people who will be a part of and benefit from your work. Before writing this off as a purely bourgeois phenomenon, consider that poor and working people's movements have for centuries relied on small donations from members. Today hundreds, if not thousands, of mass organizations of landless people, poor farmers, and subsistence wage workers all around the world fund their operations this way. In America, the internet should make it that much easier for our movements to do the same.

In 2003, Howard Dean was the first presidential candidate in American history to succeed at the long-held dream of rallying small donors to outspend the rich in campaign contributions. His online team was staffed with brilliant pioneers and constituted a "rat pack" of online campaigners including Joe Rospars, Zephyr Teachout, Michael Whitney, Nicco Mele, and many others who would go on to do great things.

As smart as they were, the fundamental force that powered their success was that Howard Dean was asking Democratic primary voters, volunteers, and donors to do some big things: repudiate decades of Clintonian "triangulation," take the party back for the "Democratic wing of the Democratic party," and "take back our country" once and for all. Whatever that meant to "Deaniacs," the ask was big, and they donated tens of millions online.

What's fascinating about developments like these, when you're involved in them as they play out in real time, is how long it takes all of us to fully realize the changes that are taking place. I helped out a little bit in the beginning—on loan from MoveOn.org, who had pioneered political email fundraising—as the Dean internet campaign was getting up and running. At one point, I drove Howard Dean from Burlington, Vermont, to Manchester, New Hampshire, to catch a plane. The first-ever "MoveOn Primary" was coming up—a survey of MoveOn.org members in which we were going to send emails from all the Democratic candidates to our entire list of several million members.

It would be the single biggest fundraising opportunity of Dean's campaign at that point in the primary—one that would continue to pay dividends over time as Dean would be able to continue to raise small-dollar contributions by email from all of the donors he gained from that first MoveOn.org fundraising email. This was before Dean had an email team—and was before anyone outside of MoveOn.org knew how to write political fundraising emails. He just happened to be sitting in a car for two hours with the one person who could help him nail this fundraising opportunity. (For the record, MoveOn.org had reached out to all the campaigns offering such help.)

I strongly believed that an authentic message from the candidate himself would make a huge difference. I raised it with him, suggesting we use the next two hours of our drive for me to help him think through the message he would write to win over MoveOn.org members.

But he had something more important to do: call time! He spent the entire trip dialing for dollars, one millionaire after another. He was calling donors who had given $1,000 or more to his campaign and asking them to "max out." And that's how he said it, "I've been told to call you and ask you to—quote—max out!" He didn't reach a single person but left a couple dozen messages on answering machines. Maybe he made a thousand dollars on that trip. What he—and his handler in the back seat—didn't know was that the email I was talking about would lead to not thousands of dollars, but millions.

These days, internet fundraising is well understood by anyone who's been paying attention. (Though it did take months of convincing before Bernie's campaign leadership finally accepted the money wasn't going to suddenly dry up.)

But if you're a grassroots activist, or a revolutionary leader in a local community, I imagine you could be looking at all of these fundraising lessons from presidential campaigns and organizations with national profiles and thinking, "What does any of this have to do with me?"

It's true that it took a lot of national campaigns over time to prime the small-dollar pump. But now all kinds of local projects are kick-started with small donations. Winning support from your community to lead a campaign or make change has never been easier.

But to raise funds this way, you need to have a base that wants to support you. If you don't have that base, you face two options: seek large donations from rich people and foundations, or build a base so you can seek small-dollar donations. There are consequences that come with each path.

If you choose the large-dollar path, the people you get money from will play a part in determining your objectives, strategies, and messaging. You will get to know them better and better, and your perspective may be influenced by them on a deeper level than you care to admit. And all of the time you spend chasing this money will be time you do not spend building your base with—and becoming more accountable to—your people.

If you choose the small-dollar path, the people you get money from will also play a part in determining your objectives, strategies, and messaging: If you find it hard to fundraise from your mass base, then probably there is a problem with your leadership or your plan or both! You will then have to keep changing until you connect with and finally communicate in a meaningful way with the people you are proposing to serve. The time you spend with your base will allow you to get to know your people better. You will be able to use that time to recruit amazing leaders out of your base. By relying on those leaders, you will find that you need fewer resources to get much more done than you could have relying solely on paid staff.

Starting out, it may be a while before you build your base and lots of small donations come pouring in. This means you'll be running an underfunded operation. But you'll be running it that way while you're building your base—instead of chasing rich people! Don't lose hope: Consider that virtually every new industrial union in the world started this way—with workers organizing and then passing the hat to collect some dues.

I worked on a project in India with some organizations whose standard source of funding staff was the following: An organization's staffer would work for free while the worker's spouse would work a "day job" to support the family. Their commitment to the cause was so deep that it was safely assumed that the spouse was all-in for this arrangement. No one ever would have considered asking for a salary—after all, the people these organizations were fighting for were typically living on the brink of starvation or working nearly every waking hour in sweatshops. If revolutionary politics in India worked the way it currently does in the US progressive movement, then those organizations would not be able to exist because the staff would be waiting on big foundations to hand out the big money to allow them to get started.

All that said, in politics, Puritanism is a bad thing! If a wealthy donor who shares your politics and respects your autonomy offers you some start-up funds, take them! If a radical foundation—and there are some—wants to support your work because it fully aligns with their mission, then accept the support. I've made ends meet a couple of times thanks to grants from foundations.

But even the most radical foundation that funds your start-up phase is going to want to rotate you out of its portfolio after a few years—that's just how foundations work. If you didn't use those few years to build an independent support base among the people you serve, then you'll find yourself begging to an inevitably less-radical foundation—a foundation that will have all kinds of time-consuming questions and concerns about the best parts of your strategies and plans.

The revolution *will* be funded—but by small donations that come from the people you serve or represent.

Barnstorm!

★ becky ★

U se mass meetings as a technology to put people to work in teams and immediately. Constantly redesign your technique to get more out of your meetings. Ensuring that your meetings can be replicated is key to scaling up for your revolution.

I thought it was a terrible idea and I didn't see how it would work. It was ludicrous on its face. But Zack was so insistent that I said let's go ahead and test it. We'd see it fail quickly, and then we could take the idea off the table and get to real solutions that would get us out of the mess we found ourselves in.

We had a big problem on our hands. There were plenty of people volunteering for Bernie, but many of them were engaged in activities that were unconnected with the campaign's plan to win.

The strategy coming down from headquarters was clear—even though some parts of the plans for implementation were not. Bernie had to win or come close to winning in those first four crucial primaries in February to prove he was a real contender for the nomination. Press coverage from his early primary wins would provide momentum to lift the campaign in the Super Tuesday states that voted March 1.

We also knew that if we had any chance at all, it was likely the election would come down to a protracted battle in later states, and that our biggest competitive advantage—after Bernie's message and his authenticity as a messenger—would be our vast army of volunteers.

But only if we could find a way to make them effective. Clinton was organizing money. We were organizing people.

That meant that Bernie volunteers who were tabling at farmers markets in Los Angeles and organizing "light brigades" in Chicago had to shift most of their energy to tasks that would impact the outcome of the election in the early primaries.

It takes time to scale up a volunteer voter contact program, and we had to get our volunteers calling voters in Iowa and the rest of the early primary states ASAP. But it wasn't as simple as sending out an email asking volunteers to log in individually from their computer and start making calls from home. From running CREDO Super-PAC's Take Down the Tea Party Ten campaign in 2012, I knew that volunteers who gathered together in person to make calls paused for less time between calls, called for more consecutive minutes, and got better faster at conversing with voters. They were also more likely to volunteer again, in part because of the accountability and camaraderie of working with fellow volunteers. To make an operation as big as we needed, we had to build a nationwide network of in-person phone banks. But of course, we didn't have field offices nationwide to host them.

There were plenty of Bernie supporters ready to get to work, and so getting people to show up in large numbers to organized phone bank events would probably be the easy part. But first we had to recruit enough people to host those voter contact events that we could then ask people to attend. The problem was that the emails we were sending to recruit phone bank hosts were tanking. Seriously tanking. Somehow, we couldn't convert the thousands of folks who had already organized debate watch parties and house parties into phone bank party hosts.

Our entire distributed organizing plan was potentially in jeopardy if we could not break through this barrier and get enough events on the map to accommodate the tens of thousands of volunteers we knew we could get involved in phone banking if only they were given a place and time to show up.

Traditionally there are two ways you get someone to say yes to a big ask like "hold a phone bank in your home." The first is to have an organizer develop volunteer leaders in-person, one-on-one, starting with small asks and then guiding them up a ladder of engagement until they were ready and willing to take on advanced tasks like organizing meetings in their homes. But we didn't even have staff on the ground in the dozens of states where the distributed team focused on organizing back in the early fall. And even if we did, it would have taken them months to generate the number of phone banks we needed operational ASAP. The most logical solution would have been to employ a typical digital strategy and just send more and better emails to get more hosts recruited online. For that to work, it would have required expanded access to Bernie's email list and more rigorous testing to find out what email format/content had the highest conversion rates.

But there were major barriers. There was already enormous pressure on the email list. Tim's team at Revolution Messaging was raising virtually all the money coming into the campaign by sending out emails. And the distributed organizing team was counting on using our weekly allotment of emails to the list to recruit volunteer leaders to set up phone banks. There wasn't enough list to go around. Then I came to learn that the software platform used by the campaign was seriously flawed when it came to how it managed distributed events. We couldn't test different email content or user flows in order to increase the conversion rate on the emails we were sending to people asking them to host events. There was no way to optimize our email recruitment program for phone bank hosts.

Zack's big idea was to get the digital organizing staff out from behind our computers and travel around the country holding big, in-person meetings with Bernie supporters. We'd turn the one-on-one on its head by organizing lots of people simultaneously through big, powerful, in-person meetings that put people to work immediately. In these mass meetings we could strong-arm volunteers into hosting phone banks. If the meetings were big enough, it would be worth it.

It would work in part because the meeting would be just part of what we digital types on the distributed organizing team called the "user flow." The meeting would be part of a chain of interactions with the volunteers that flowed from online to an in-person meeting to the phone and back online. For example, we could follow up by phone and email to convert anyone who held a single phone bank into a host that held recurring weekly events. So for every host recruited, that meant the possibility of dozens of future phone banks.

That said, we had an email list with millions of supporters on it. We had a ton of daily tasks that would be disrupted by traveling to venues to hold events. How could flying to a city and having an in-person meeting to recruit volunteers really be more efficient than sending lots more email from Burlington?

We would soon find out. Zack and Corbin scheduled a series of meetings they called "barnstorms" across Tennessee over a three-day period in late October. The email invitations simply said that Zack Exley and Corbin Trent from the national staff of the Bernie campaign were heading to their towns, and they were invited to learn directly from the campaign how they could get to work to help elect Bernie president of the United States. From Memphis to Denver to Austin, volunteers turned out in droves to these meetings. Even meetings in small towns like Johnson City, Tennessee, brought out 150 people. In a big city like Austin, we could easily assemble three hundred people if the venue were big enough.

So Zack was right. We could create the wide end of a conversion funnel with the barnstorm meeting. We could assemble a lot of people in one place with a single email. Once the email went out, some of the people who received it would post the event to local Bernie Facebook groups and other social platforms. The local super volunteers who were connected to each other would do the rest of the recruitment work for us. While we started out with a traditional email sequence of invitation, reminder, and then follow up, we soon came to realize that we didn't even have to ask for RSVPs or send email follow-up reminders and instead could launch these mass meetings with just one email. (Later on we started using peer-to-peer texting when pressure on the email list made it even more difficult to schedule event recruitment. In Oklahoma City, Bernie staffer Pete D'Alessandro, who helped win an upset in the Oklahoma primary by a massive margin, turned out nearly four hundred people using individually sent text messages.)

Getting people to show up in large numbers was only part of the challenge. We needed to get volunteers all the way through the conversion funnel and out the other end to doing real work that mattered. With so much staff time invested in traveling to and attending a meeting in person, we had to figure out how to achieve a high conversion rate on phone banks created. With this we were working against history. The mass meeting was traditionally seen as what we would call a "low-bar ask" on the ladder of engagement, and the organizing outcome was usually a list of interested people who a staffer would then follow up with individually in the weeks following the meeting. To make Zack's plan work, we needed at least 10 percent of the people at the meeting to commit to holding phone banks and more than half of the remaining people to sign up to be the core attendees for these events, which we would also then promote to other area supporters online.

We had to figure this out and figure it out quickly, as we couldn't spend staff time running meetings unless they could consistently generate a massive number of volunteer voter contact shifts. So we approached these barnstorm mass meetings like any other channel for interaction within the distributed organizing program. It would be designed, managed, iterated, reinvented, and scaled like other essential technologies that mediated exchanges between supporters and the campaign.

Our requirements for the meeting were that it had to be replicable, low cost, and result in the highest possible conversion rates in response to our organizing asks. What resulted from months of testing and reinvention was a scripted, ninety-minute, in-person meeting—supported by a dozen national volunteer-led support teams—where supporters were invited to learn about campaign strategy and to find out how they could step up to be volunteer leaders, and then to sign up for actual shifts where they would do valuable work to win the campaign.

When Zack and I explain this strategy to other folks who work in digital, we call it a logical extension of the campaign's UI, or user interface, into the real world, optimized for the highest conversion rate of the in-person interaction. When we discuss it with old-school organizers, we say we are replacing Alinsky's model based on one-on-ones and a ladder of engagement with a mass meeting where everyone gets to work right there. However you come to understand this tactic, we want you to understand it as a linchpin of big organizing and a rule that could change everything in how you approach your work.

Mass meetings for organizing are not pep rallies. Their purpose is not to educate people on the issues. They are a tool for putting people who are already on your list to work on valuable tasks that will help you execute a strategic campaign plan.

As we've said before, on the Bernie campaign, our greatest asset was always Bernie's message. The second-best asset was Bernie as the messenger running in all fifty states for the presidential nomination. People who came to the meeting had already been organized to take action by Bernie—they didn't need to be educated or motivated. The goal of the meeting's agenda was to put people already inspired to take action into teams where they could do meaningful work to help Bernie win.

Bringing people together in person, communicating the national strategy to volunteers, and then explaining the concrete roles they needed to play in that strategy for it to succeed was how we moved people from feeling inspired to doing valuable work. Whether it's fighting fracking in your state or blocking ICE from breaking up families with senseless deportations, there are people who are knowledgeable about the issues and ready to take action to change the status quo. They don't need an organizer to tell them why they should get involved. They want to get to work to make real change. The mass meeting should be designed with these people in mind.

No matter what part of the political revolution you are working to build, you will have to constantly iterate and reinvent your mass meetings to optimize for success. In our first barnstorm meetings in October, we learned how to get hundreds of people together who wanted to get to work. But it took a couple dozen meetings—in places like Johnson City, Tennessee; St. Louis, Missouri; and Colorado Springs, Colorado—to figure out how to get enough of the people assembled to commit to holding a phone bank at a specific time and place. Once we figured this out and optimized for it, we could successfully roll into a city like Seattle, where in December, 2015, we assembled five hundred people at Town Hall Seattle, and recruited eighty phone bank party hosts during our ninety-minute meeting.

But at this point, we were being forced to recognize another problem that had been mounting as we held more and more barnstorms. Once people understood the plan to achieve the big goal, they were willing to volunteer to do the big things we asked of them. The barnstorms were putting a huge number of events on the map at map.berniesanders.com. We assumed that once phone banks were there, the emails would work their usual magic and people would sign up and fill them to capacity. But in reality, all along at this early stage, many of the phone banks we were creating on the road got zero online signups. Or sometimes more awkwardly for volunteers who had never met before, just one person would attend.

We had to come to terms with this in Seattle when eighty phone bank hosts filled the Seattle Area with their events—a new record—and the number of people we could turn out by email would be spread too thin across all those phone banks. We had created too many! We had optimized a powerful machine for creating volunteer leaders, and we had neglected to put mechanisms in place to recruit other volunteers to join their teams.

It felt awful. We had set up these volunteer leaders to fail. But that was a necessary part of the process. The distributed team had gathered in person in Seattle for a kick-off summit to get ready for the sprint to the Iowa caucus. Claire Sandberg, Saikat Chakrabarti, and Sam Briggs, a veteran field organizer who had just joined the campaign, talked about the RSVP crisis over dinner. They came to a conclusion that now seems obvious—that we stop depending on email for the RSVPs and instead have the audience sign up on the spot for volunteer leaders' phone bank events. We were already having to do data entry of the forms with the created events. Why not also have people sign up on the forms and have volunteers manually enter that into the campaign database. If conversion rates went up enough, it would be worth the volunteer work to do the additional data entry.

When they brought this idea back to the whole team, Corbin and Zack said that from their experiences on the road it would be impossible to choreograph the match-making between hosts and attendees who lived nearby. In a crowded room it was hard enough to get at least one out of ten participants to fill out the form to create an event. How would attendees figure out which sign-up sheet was for the event closest to them and on a date they could attend. It would be like a cross between a rugby scrum and a chaotic game of Twister. But everyone agreed, we needed to figure it out or we were wasting our time doing barnstorms.

For the next couple of weeks, a bunch of staffers, including Zack and me, tested different ways of signing up phone bank attendees. We discussed our failures on conference calls and on Slack. How would we connect the phone bank hosts who stood up at the barnstorms with the supporters in the audience who wanted to sign up for their events when there were hundreds of people in the room? One early test had to do with holding aloft handmade signs taped to the top of wooden yard sticks. We'll spare you all the gory details of that and other attempts to solve this problem, but imagine my dismay when I arrived with Zack at an airport at Kansas City as we traveled from barnstorm to barnstorm and Zack actually wanted (and eventually succeeded in convincing) the United agent to allow him to check a bundle of fifty wooden yard sticks clumsily bound up in adhesive tape! This was simply not going to work.

Through trial and error, we figured it out. The solution was an "altar call" where phone bank hosts lined up at the front of the meeting and did a lightning round of pitches for their events. We told the audience to remember the person who was holding their phone bank at a location, date, and time that was convenient for them, and then when all the hosts had pitched (sometimes as many as forty of them!), we told everyone to get up and go find the host they had picked, and get their name on that person's form. It was pandemonium every time, but it worked!

Your leadership ask may not be to get someone to volunteer to lead a weekly phone bank, but whatever your organizing goal is, any organizer developing a powerful mass meeting for their cause will have to iterate—and be honest with your supporters—that you are trying to figure things out and improve as you go. Our supporters stuck with us despite the chaos because they knew that if we were going to help Bernie win, we had to build the biggest campaign ever seen in presidential primary history. And once we perfected the method, our numbers shot up.

Here are some elements that made our barnstorms successful.

- The meeting needs to have a clear and coherent agenda and end on time. A volunteer's time is valuable and should be respected. An organizer's time is always in short supply and should be maximized by keeping meetings efficient.

- There needs to be a system to stop blowhards from hijacking meetings, alienating volunteers who want to get to work, and wasting people's time. The majority of people who are attending the meeting want to get to work. Issue debates or personal agendas can be entertained after the meeting is done and people are free to go.

- The organizer should lay out a clear campaign strategy that is heavy on tactics, timeline, and a concrete path to victory, and light (if addressed at all) on explaining the issues, providing inspiration, or engaging in punditry.

- The organizer should shift the interaction of the web sign-up process into the real world to dramatically increase conversion—with manual intervention by volunteers to get the sign-ups back online. To do this, there must be an in-person sign-up form that is treated as a valuable technology, tweaks to which can have a dramatic impact on conversion rates.

- A strong and specific ask will get people get committed and prepared to do actual work in teams formed right on the spot. Ask who can lead events and have them agree to a time and date on the spot. Write it down on a piece of paper with room for others to RSVP. Then have the hosts announce their events one at a time and ask everyone else in the meeting to sign up for their event right there. Aim for 10–20 percent of the room to step up as volunteer leaders, and 70–80 percent of the room to sign up to join their teams. This makes everyone accountable not just to the campaign but to each other in a real and personal way.

- There should be a support layer of people, processes, and software. Engaging volunteers in work at a mass meeting isn't simply a handshake between a website process, an invitation to volunteers, a tested meeting agenda, and set of paper forms. It depends on layers of volunteer support teams connected by social platforms and the campaign's central organizing technology to do the data entry, follow up with hosts, send reminder RSVPs to make sure the work happens, and track the vital statistics for the relationship between the meetings held, organizing events planned, and volunteer shifts completed.

By January, barnstorm meetings were responsible for creating the majority of distributed phone banks for the Bernie campaign. To put the impact of the barnstorms in context, when we held our first Arizona barnstorm meeting using this model in a union hall in Phoenix, the state director, Jose Miranda, remarked afterward that we created more phone banks in ninety minutes then he could have in three weeks of full-time work. He mentioned that a supporter who had turned him down to host a phone bank in a one-on-one in the past had stepped up and volunteered to host at the barnstorm. Jose was a great organizer. He was one of our best state directors. It wasn't that he wasn't already doing everything right. It was that the barnstorm model was that powerful.

Making the barnstorm replicable was one of our key requirements for our approach to the meeting as technology. This led to the most important breakthrough—recruiting and training volunteers to lead these meetings instead of staff. The first volunteer training for leading barnstorms was conducted in Austin, Texas, just over a week before the Iowa caucus. Volunteer leaders matched or exceeded conversion rates for meeting attendance, hosts, and RSVPs to future voter contact events. Training of barnstorm hosts was moved to YouTube livestream events and eventually 650 of the campaign's 1,000 barnstorm meetings were led by volunteers.

We considered the barnstorm meeting the most valuable innovation devised by our department over the course of the campaign. We

82

love that one of the biggest tech innovations by a bunch of digital organizers involved big, in-person, mass meetings. Being part of the Bernie campaign was a constant exercise in throwing out the conventional wisdom and trying unlikely approaches until you found the vehicle that could scale volunteer impact big enough to go toe to toe with the billionaire-backed candidates.

Fight the Tyranny of the Annoying

★ becky ★

Don't let well-intentioned but ultimately disruptive activists drive good people away from the movement! Sometimes, the worst person with the most time on his hands ends up dominating a group and scaring off exactly the kind of people you're trying to attract. Even when they mean well, it's important to ask these people to leave your groups, and to develop a culture where they won't be allowed to derail the revolution.

Zack is someone who finds great joy in meeting new people, learning their stories, figuring out what's uniquely wonderful about them, and then getting to work together for a common purpose. He's part coach, part cheerleader, part evangelist, and 100 percent the person you'd want to be in a foxhole with. Only someone like Zack could cheerfully articulate the rule that we have to fight the tyranny of the annoying.

You probably have experienced the tyranny of the annoying. It's when a group of people come together to work for change, and the worst person with the most time on his hands (and it's usually a guy but not always, of course) ends up dominating the group and driving others away.

That's the tyranny of the annoying, and we have to fight it. Because what could be worse than good people being driven away from the movement?

When we organize, we strive to create the conditions that allow people to work together to win the change they want to see in the world. It could be neighbors coming together to campaign for a stop sign at a dangerous intersection. It could be people who want to keep fossil fuels in the ground and so are working to block an oil export terminal. At its heart, organizing is about helping people build power, and the best way to do this is together. But what happens when the most annoying person hijacks the group?

Over the past century, there's been an overall decline in civic and social organization—documented by academics such as Theda Skocpol and Robert Putnam. It's true we have seen some surges in big organizing—immigration activists fighting and winning deportation relief for Dreamers, the climate defenders stopping infrastructure like the Keystone XL pipeline and pushing to keep fossil fuels in the ground, and the movement to defend black lives fighting to hold cops accountable for murdering black people with impunity and unelecting some county prosecutors in the process. But in recent decades, a lot of activism has been trending in two decidedly smaller directions: small-dollar fundraising to pay professional activists to advocate on issues or otherwise run campaigns that are not volunteer driven; and internet-enabled activism that drives large numbers of people to take small, relatively unconnected individual actions to weigh in with corporate or governmental decision makers, a form of organizing that avoids people ever having to work together.

Based on our experience as organizers, one of the drivers of this change is the tyranny of the annoying.

What's so heartening about the work of organizing is that most people who want to make a difference are wonderful. But what inspires dread in us is that one person in one hundred who, for whatever reason, has a need for attention, control, and conflict—and has enough time on his hands to wear everyone else down and eventually take over a group, dominate it, and drive others away.

One of Zack's first encounters with the tyranny of the annoying was at a small campaign finance reform group when he was a college student in western Massachusetts. Every week, one or two new good people would show up to get involved. But they almost never returned. It's a really great story as Zack tells it. "Maybe it had something to do with a seventy-five-year-old man who was a regular at these meetings." According to Zack, he rarely bathed, treated people rudely, and in the middle of each meeting would open up a container of rancid vegetables that he would proceed to eat, causing on at least one occasion a prospective member to audibly gag. After finishing his meal, this man would pull out some dental floss and clean his teeth, flicking bits of rotting broccoli all over the table and sometimes onto one of the newbies sitting next to him (Zack promises that last part is not an exaggeration and that he was personally struck by rotting broccoli bits). But the really important thing to mention here is the way that this man fought to dominate meetings, making them boring and unproductive.

Now, to be clear: We really love people like the activist described. According to Zack, this man was a character who had been making trouble for decades. He was a well-known labor and antiwar activist. He was a wonderful person. But he had issues that prevented him from behaving as a member of a group should—and he had behavior patterns that drove people away from any ordinary public gathering that he was a part of.

As an organizer, you're supposed to love everybody (at least everybody on your side). That's part of what makes fighting the tyranny of the annoying so hard. It means dealing with disruptive people so that the rest of the folks who are ready to get to work can spend their time on productive and often fun organizing tasks. Sometimes that means asking the annoying person to accept some boundaries, sometimes it means asking them to leave, other times it means actually telling them to leave.

One of the rules we had on the campaign—and this came from Bernie—is that organizers never said anything negative about Clinton. In our distributed organizing communications, we didn't even name her—we would contrast Bernie's stances on the issues to the "billionaire-backed candidates."

At my first barnstorm, in Colorado Springs, a very well put together woman in her seventies approached me before the meeting to let me know that she had a personal story to share that attested to Clinton's "disgusting" corruption. She looked every bit the retired attorney she claimed to be and her information pertained to a court case she said she and Bernie's opponent had been personally involved in. I politely explained that our meeting was for people who wanted to get to work and we wouldn't be having discussions about Clinton. I went even further to say that Bernie himself had instructed us NOT to discuss the Clinton campaign but instead focus on solutions. I thought we were good.

There were around 150 people in attendance that night at the Lon Chaney Theater in downtown Colorado Springs. Soon after opening the meeting, we asked a few members of the audience who were new to organizing to tell the story of how they came to support Bernie. Somehow, the supporter with the burning need to share her personal testimony to Hillary Clinton's corruption got hold of a microphone. This professional retiree launched into a vitriolic diatribe about Clinton's allegedly nefarious dealings in an obscure court case that she had personal knowledge of. I practically sprinted to the back of the audience and proceeded to physically eject this passionate, pro-Bernie senior after she rejected my requests to hand back the mic!

I felt horrible, but I also knew that if I didn't deal with the situation, there might be five or ten valuable minutes of the meeting that we could never get back. Think about it. One-hundred fifty people in the room. One person, no matter how well meaning, had hijacked our agenda. While five minutes seems like a small amount of time, multiply that by the 149 other people who were there to get to work and you've wasted over twelve hours of the audience's combined time. And it was not just the hijacking of time but also the hijacking of the spirit of the meeting. We had so much positive stuff to plan, and we all knew why we were for Bernie and not his opponent.

It can feel terrible to shut down a volunteer who almost always has the best of intentions. It can feel even worse to fire someone from a volunteer team who is committed and putting in a lot of hours but

ultimately is too disruptive to others to stay on the team. No organizer wants to play the oppressor by singling someone out in a group
in an avowedly antiauthoritarian audience, but sometimes that's
exactly what an organizer has to do. In reality you aren't oppressing
someone—you're liberating the rest of the group. Professional progressive organizers in particular tend to be polite and want to avoid
conflict. Too often that means avoiding organizing people to work
together in real life in favor of alternative forms of activism that don't
require joint, in-person action.

At the beginning of our barnstorms, it really energized the room
to hear a few members of the audience say why they had joined
the campaign. Zack came up with a revelatory way to prevent the
tyranny of the annoying from popping up in that part of the over
one thousand barnstorm meetings we organized. It was brilliant
because it was so simple. In the barnstorm instructions, we required
organizers to ask the audience to raise their hands if they were new
to campaigning. More than half of the room inevitably raised their
hands. While those hands were up, we would pick out a few to call
on to share their story of why they were getting involved with the
Bernie campaign.

In the barnstorm instructions we wrote:

- Make sure you deliberately call on specific people. Don't
  lose control of the mic, whether that's a real mic or just
  control of the room.
- Choose people who are often excluded from the political
  process: women, people of color, and very young people.
  Their stories are often the most powerful.
- If someone starts going on for a long time, politely ask them
  to wrap up. If they continue going on, ask them to stop and
  call on someone else to speak. This isn't a time for extended
  discussions of strategy, messaging, or political ideology—
  it's a time to share personal stories with the group.

But when we personally trained staff, we got practical and simply
said, "Always call on people new to politics who are women, people

of color, or the youngest people in the room." When we followed this to the letter, we almost always got short, inspirational, authentic personal stories. When we didn't, we inevitably ended up with a white guy on the mic wasting another twelve hours of collective volunteer time going on a political tirade that, while important to him, was not what others were attending the meeting to hear.

That's what Lilia Villa, a digital nerd from Chico, California, encountered when she helped lead a barnstorm in a church in the town of Richmond, California. Lilia postponed her wedding to the woman she loved and set aside a thriving tech consulting business to join the digital organizing team. She was a true believer among true believers.

Richmond was a place of significance for us, and we were quite honored to be holding a barnstorm there. It is the San Francisco Bay Area site of the Chevron Richmond Refinery that has been responsible for a series of chemical leaks, gas releases, and a 1993 gas explosion that created what has been called a mini-Bhopal. In the 2014 election, Chevron spent over $3 million trying to defeat progressives on the Richmond city council who had been working to hold the nation's third richest company accountable for damaging the economy and environment of this town of one hundred thousand.

Bernie had visited Richmond shortly before the election to campaign against Chevron's corporate takeover attempt and to rally his local supporters against Citizens United. The voters he rallied helped progressive crusaders Jovanka Beckles and Eduardo Martinez overcome $3 million in corporate money and win four-year terms on the city council.

Jovanka and Eduardo were there at the barnstorm to show solidarity with Bernie for the help he had given them, and to sign up as many people as possible to work in Bernie's political revolution. I was there with Lilia and it was an honor to get to meet these progressive fighters, and to speak with a crowd of Bernie supporters who didn't just believe that people power could defeat the corporate interests— they knew it because they had done it just two years before.

It was near the beginning of the meeting and Lilia had warmed up the crowd. More than half the people in the room raised their hands when she asked who was campaigning for a politician for the very first time. When she asked how many people had given money to Bernie, nearly 80 percent of the hands shot up. Then she asked the crowd that had donated to keep their hands up if this had been their first donation to a candidate ever. Nearly half of the donations were from new people.

Then came the moment when she asked for a few people who were new to campaigns to share with us why they were supporting Bernie. These statements sometimes brought tears. "I lost my house, while the bankers got bonuses. Bernie is going to help people like me." Or "I'm here because my eighteen-year-old son got me involved. He thinks Bernie can change things." Or "My daughter just started college, and my husband and I are still paying off our college loans. Something has to change."

The hands went up. Mostly older white guys. Lilia looked around the room and then she called on one of them! He was passionate and well meaning. But he talked for a long time, delivering the kind of negatively tinged and yet incredibly detailed political analysis that tends to turn off the newcomers we were counting on to make things different this time. We don't mean to disparage white men. And please don't worry: We were not silencing them; many white men at pretty much every single organizing meeting definitely had their say in the Q&A and discussion. In fact, they often interrupted us without being called on while we were talking!

It's up to all of us to fight the tyranny of the annoying. Because organizing loses when we retreat solely into tactics that protect us from being annoyed—like fundraising, professional advocacy, or internet-enabled petitioning. We need all of our tactics to be on the table. We can't let a handful of people psyche us out. We have to fight the tyranny of the annoying because the highest calling of an organizer is not to help people by winning victories for them, it's to help people work together to build their own power and make change.

Give Away Your Passwords

★ becky ★

E mbrace risk in order to get as many people involved as possible and let them organize as constituencies with their own voices. Radical trust, with some limits, can build community that scales.

In this book we're talking about the rules for revolution that we learned not just during our time as distributed organizers on the Bernie campaign, but over four decades of our combined experience in organizing.

Zack and I knew that conventional campaigns would never be big enough to elect Bernie president so, together with the distributed organizing team, we sought to test counterintuitive strategies that promised big gains, leading to rules like "The revolution will not be staffed" and "Barnstorm!" Of course, it wasn't just us. We were in the midst of a sea change and weren't the only people trying to jettison the old orthodoxies that were forcing small organizing on a movement that needed (and wanted) to be big. There was a new and independent force on social media: The People for Bernie.

Some of the defining message moments of Bernie's run came not from the campaign but from The People for Bernie community. It was The People for Bernie who first spied a photo of Bernie sitting in a middle seat flying coach back in December, 2015, in the Bernie subreddit and decided to memeify it with the headline: "I'm voting for the guy willing to sit in the middle seat." The meme went viral. And of course, the founders will go down in history as the people who popularized the hashtag that came to define the campaign first on social media and then in the real world on everything from T-shirts to street murals to tattoos: #FeelTheBern.

The People for Bernie was founded back in April of 2015 by a couple of professional digital troublemakers, Winnie Wong and Charles Lenchner. Winnie was a founding member of Occupy Wall Street. Charles cut his teeth in presidential campaigning on the Dennis Kucinich campaign back in 2003. Both were among the drivers behind the early grassroots attempt "Ready for Warren" to draft Elizabeth Warren into the presidential primary (Ready for Warren preceded the more institutional "Run Warren Run" campaign launched by MoveOn.org and Democracy for America).

They launched the community with an open letter from veteran grassroots organizers of Occupy Wall Street, as well as fellow travelers in movements for "peace, rights, and the planet." Together, they were answering Bernie's call to work for solutions that were as radical as the problems we face, and they invited others from the left flank of the progressive movement to join them. Then they set out to build a social media juggernaut with a bigger reach than the campaign's official presence on Facebook.

The People for Bernie was tailor-made to make a presidential campaign nervous. Here was this independent social media empire with Bernie's name on it run by people who were totally unaccountable and uncontrollable. No one was funding them, so no one could tell them what to do (and more important, what not to do!). They were posting memes about Hillary Clinton when Bernie staffers had explicit instructions not to be negative about the Clintons on social media. Also, The People for Bernie kept expanding into constituency groups that the campaign didn't even have official staff assigned to. They were running out ahead of us and outflanking us with new social media properties like African Americans for Bernie and Millennials for Bernie. And they were getting news coverage.

Charles and Winnie both rebelled against the completely normal campaign mindset that certain things had to be tightly controlled, like messaging, data, and access to senior staff. They embraced the big organizing tenant of trusting in more people more often. They also embraced risk in order to make sure there was room for everybody. Which is why they gave away the passwords.

Back in April when The People for Bernie launched on Facebook, Winnie Wong created a host of other pages: Latinos for Bernie, Moms for Bernie, African Americans for Bernie, Jews for Bernie, Socialists for Bernie, Asian Americans for Bernie. The list of social media properties goes on. Winnie and Charles thought that everyone should be able to bring their authentic self to building a movement behind the Bernie candidacy, and they knew speed, depth, and breadth was of the essence. But how were two people going to curate and manage so many iterations of these dynamic communities of Bernie supporters?

That's when they started to give away the passwords.

Giving away the passwords is a metaphor for the radical trust and community building that The People for Bernie brought to their brand of big organizing. But it wasn't anarchy. Like most big organizing, it was structured, it used social platforms to help it scale, and it sought to get as many people involved as possible, instead of just a desired few.

After they sent out the open letter in late April, The People for Bernie community was small but growing. Winnie and Charles sent out a Facebook invitation to attend a conference call where interested, movement-oriented folks could learn how to help build out the community on social media. The primary channel for this invitation was the one million people who liked Occupy Wall Street on Facebook. RSVPs started coming in. First there were one hundred, then five hundred, and eventually over one thousand people joined the call.

They were prepared for the onslaught of eager volunteer leaders. They'd already been using a conference call product called Maestro via InterOccupy, the online hub where the Occupy movement shifted to collaborate and organize after Zuccotti Park. The call was no navel-gazing hippy confab. There was an introduction. A seasoned facilitator from Occupy who goes by the name Jack Rabbit led a discussion about why everyone had come together and why specifically they were supporting Bernie. Winnie and Charles explained how people could get to work, and then the invitation was issued: If you're interested in organizing social media groups by constituency, press 1 on your phone. About a hundred of those who pressed 1 ended up in a private conference call "room" with Winnie.

What happened next was the kind of thing that no official campaign ever could have done with its messaging—but it parallels our initiatives of building volunteer teams to run vital infrastructure. Winnie started with ten constituency communities she had set up on Facebook: Asian Americans for Bernie, Jews for Bernie, Vets for Bernie, and so on. Then she explained what the process would be for "handing over the keys" to these pages on Facebook and asked people who were interested in being administrators to email her directly and let her know what constituency group they could help lead. Then she spent a little time getting to know people. To those she trusted, she sent out a document with a set of ground rules for managing the account, including how to construct a post, how many times per day to post, and perhaps most importantly what not to post. She also sent out a password for a Dropbox account that she had preloaded with images they could use to customize their pages. People who made it all the way through the process were given passwords and empowered to go out and do the work. She continued to mentor the new administrators, offering follow-up training calls on social media and checking in to make sure pages were being updated. When posting slowed down, she'd simply start again and recruit new administrators through the exact same process.

One of the people on that first call was Moumita Ahmed, a young activist from Queens, New York. She had worked on Zephyr Teachout's campaign for governor as a field organizer and would go on to be the influential cofounder of Millennials for Bernie Sanders and a national organizer for The People for Bernie. Millennials for Bernie Sanders—which was later rebranded as Millennials for Revolution—became a powerful platform that catapulted Moumita to national prominence as a spokesperson for young people supporting Bernie's message of revolution both during and after the primary. Moumita traveled to volunteer on the ground in a few primaries, then got hired to work on the New York State primary in the month before the election—the exciting campaign that activists would call "The Battle of New York."

It was working. Winnie and her fellow Occupy alums were methodically recreating many of the best elements of the town square that happened in-person at Zuccotti Park, on the internet. They entertained, educated, and motivated countless numbers of Bernie supporters, with the explicit goal of then migrating them from online engagement to offline volunteering via the campaign's own distributed voter contact programs.

The People for Bernie was an almost perfect social media storm, massive in reach, cutting edge in content, and breathtakingly diverse in the communities it engaged—faithfully living up to its name: *The People* for Bernie. With outrageous levels of shares, posts, comments, and likes on Facebook (all of those add up to the number of people who engaged the content—The People for Bernie's social media content hit timelines literally billions of times) it was also an important counterbalance to the corporate mainstream media that essentially ignored the Bernie campaign for much of the cycle.

The idea behind sharing rules for revolutionaries is to take this amazing movement moment that millions of people were a part of (and so many others watched from the sidelines) and set out a new marker for what big organizing can make possible as the political revolution continues beyond the Bernie campaign. The People for Bernie truly inspired us to stretch even beyond what we'd done in the campaign to give away the passwords and put the people in charge of defining the campaign's messages, personalizing it across all communities, and building a powerful alternative to (though not a replacement for) the mainstream media.

Don't Let the Perfect Be the Enemy of the Big

★ becky ★

I f you want to be perfect, your reach will be limited by your budget. To go big you need to hand over control of key work, education, and management processes to volunteers.

The organizing we did on the Bernie campaign wasn't big just because it was a presidential campaign. It was big because we built the distributed arm of the campaign to allow volunteers to scale up their own work.

After the Democratic National Convention, Zack and I attended a meeting in Berlin for organizers fighting fascism across Europe, in Scandinavia, and as far away as in India, New Zealand, and South Africa. They had all followed the Bernie campaign with keen interest. We talked with them about how they could take some of the lessons from the Bernie campaign and fight smarter and bigger in their own countries. We talked with them at length about two rules: "Get on the phone!" and "Barnstorm!" Both of these rules are about engaging volunteers and putting them to work. This idea intrigued them. Avijit Michael, a cofounder of the Indian grassroots campaigning organization Jhatkaa, asked what was seemingly on everyone's mind. How could he trust volunteers not to do something to tarnish the grassroots brand he and fellow staff were painstakingly trying to build into a trusted force for change? What if the volunteers messed up and it made the organization look bad?

I'd already connected with Avi the day before when he made a point of telling me that the first online action he'd ever taken was with CREDO. I told him that I understood how scary it was to put your brand in the hands of volunteers because we were also hyper sensitive about our brand at CREDO, especially because we were a company with a product the revenue from which supported our social change work. If customers thought we were doing a poor job based on something a volunteer did, it wasn't just an end-of-year donation we were putting at risk. Our customers paid their CREDO cell phone bills every month—that's like a huge recurring donation!

I explained that at CREDO and at Bernie we used this rule. I explained that you have to make a decision. Do you want to be perfect? Or do you need to be big? Sometimes you need to be big in order to win. If you want to be big and you can't afford to pay everybody you need to get there, you have to accept that giving volunteers responsibility means that things won't always turn out exactly the way you want them to all of the time. That said, by scaling with volunteers doing valuable work, you'll get far more work done, and that will mean a large net gain even when all the work isn't perfect.

I suggested doing what we did at CREDO when working with volunteers: manage to an 80–20 split. That means 80 percent of what you do has to be good or great. And then be okay with it if 20 percent turns out to be not so good and maybe once in a while something is horrible. If you can allow yourself to let mistakes happen (but not too many!) in order to scale up, you'll end up ahead. And don't forget, paid staff aren't perfect, either!

Of course, some things are too important for the 80–20 rule. We didn't suggest that volunteers run a national press operation. If volunteers got the message and execution wrong even 20 percent of the time talking to the national campaign press corps, that would be a disaster, but we did have an 80–20 rule for events. Usually I think we were hitting more like 95–5 because volunteers are generally amazing if you trust them to do meaningful work.

On Bernie, it wasn't always perfect. Only a handful of times—out of thousands—we'd invite our supporters to go to a volunteer-led event and the volunteer who was supposed to be in charge didn't show up. There was also the *one* guy who hosted a phone bank in his apartment in New York City. When volunteers who signed up online showed up, there was porn on the TV and the guy was smoking weed. But that's not the worst thing. He tried to charge people for attending his volunteer phone bank! Of course the volunteers reported this to the campaign and we blocked him from posting any future events. But most of the time the gatherings were wonderful and volunteers did a better job than staff might have done. Volunteers certainly tended to provide better food!

When Zack and I were at MoveOn.org and CREDO respectively, the 80–20 rule came into play occasionally, but on Bernie it became an important norm 24/7 in our corner of the campaign. It taught me that I had to embrace risk and let more things happen that might not turn out to be perfect along the way in order to get as many people involved as possible.

On the Bernie campaign, our work built upon, but was different from, the amazing and groundbreaking organizing done by Obama in 2008. Obama in 2008 had something we didn't have enough of on the Bernie campaign—with some great exceptions like our Iowa, New Hampshire, and advance teams. A true commitment to quality management of staff at all levels on the Obama campaign had a tremendous impact on the discipline, morale, and overall effectiveness of the staff. Those well-trained, well-managed staff members in turn managed volunteer teams in a way that reflected the priorities that organizing legends like Jeremy Bird, Jon Carson, Joy Cushman, Peachy Meyers, and Buffy Wicks designed into the DNA of their field campaign.

On Bernie, it was messy. Whereas the Obama campaign was obsessed with training and coaching, the Bernie campaign had very little—or no—training for staff. In the distributed program, of course, our ratio of staff to volunteers was crazy big. We were never perfect. Not even close! This was in part because at every step of the way we had to choose whether we wanted something to be perfect or whether we needed it to be big. On our team, the answer was always that we needed it to be big.

As late as December 2015, our team was tasked with organizing the volunteers in forty-some-odd states because few of the Super

Tuesday state directors had yet been hired. There were eleven of us, a mix of professional organizers and super volunteers who had just been brought onto a campaign payroll for the first time in their lives.

Like a typical digital operation, no one had prioritized meeting in person, though we were spending hours together on Slack and in conference calls. Ceci had the idea that we should get together in advance of the sprint to Iowa. We knew our ability to organize would slow down over the Christmas and New Year's holidays. But then starting January 2, the media would whip people into a frenzy around the countdown to the "first in the nation" Iowa caucuses on February 1. We decided to get everyone together in Seattle since a few of us were based on the West Coast and we had barnstorm events scheduled in the Pacific Northwest.

On December 12, we assembled in Seattle where Ceci convinced a Bernie supporter who worked at a hotel to give us a supercheap deal. Part of what we needed to do in five days of meetings was to simply get to know each other. Crucially, we needed to figure out how to work effectively as a team. We still hadn't set ground rules for things like when people on the West Coast needed to be available for meeting with Burlington-based staff. Or what the expectations were for how meetings would be run. And, of course, everyone had to be oriented around a central plan.

That plan at its heart was to get as many people as possible involved in voter contact, and staff all the support teams necessary to scale the voter machine up so that it could handle as many volunteers as we could convince to call voters in the early states. We didn't have any numerical goals from field. We didn't know when people in the Super Tuesday states should start calling their own voters or whether everybody should be doing Iowa until we ran out of numbers. We didn't begrudge the traditional field leaders for not taking our program seriously—after all, nothing like it had existed in a presidential primary before. We knew that we needed to prove to them that we could make huge numbers of voter contacts first, before we'd have a right to expect to be included.

Claire, Zack, and I huddled together to discuss presenting a big goal to the group in the absence of goals given to us by field. I insisted that it be big and motivating and just shy of feeling impossible to reach. Claire crunched some numbers on volunteer shifts she thought we could organize on a weekly basis and came up with a stretch goal of ninety thousand conversations with voters in the first four primaries, with an intense focus on Iowa, before February 1. I said, "Well, if you're already at ninety thousand, might as well make it a nice, round one hundred thousand."

Claire rolled out the goal to the group. Based on the calling we'd been organizing to that point, where every volunteer manually dials every number on their own phone, this goal was impossible. It wasn't that we couldn't get volunteers to dial one hundred thousand numbers. A focused volunteer could hand-dial about eighty to one hundred numbers an hour. It was that with this manual system each volunteer was only talking to three or four voters an hour. The area code wasn't local, which could dissuade people from picking up. You had to wait for the phone to ring, which took time. If you got an answering machine, you had to hang up. And even if someone answered the phone, it might not be the person you were hoping to talk with. If we only reached four voters per volunteer hour, we were talking about generating twenty-five thousand hours of volunteer calling to reach the one hundred thousand calls goal. Not only was that not really possible to hit—it would be a miserable experience for the volunteers. Morale was already suffering from the low contact rates on the manual dialing. At barnstorms it was becoming typical for one or two volunteers to tell the crowd how inefficient phone banking was and to urge us to find a different ask. There would have been a mutiny if we tried to ram through so many shifts through brute force.

The answer was using a technology called a dialer. From before the time I'd joined the campaign, I'd been pushing Zack—and then Zack and Claire—on the need to add a web-based dialer to our tools for volunteers. It was essential to scaling up a voter contact program of any significance outside of brick-and-mortar offices.

With a web-based dialer, a software platform dials a long list of numbers instead of having the user dial every number individually on the phone. The software can differentiate between a human answering the phone and a voice-mail message and only connects the call to the volunteer once an actual person picks up. This saves the users from having to dial a bunch of numbers that won't be picked up. Instead, they dial in once, sit on the line, and wait for live calls to be connected to them as soon as someone picks up. When they get connected with a call, a screen pops up on their computer letting them know who the person is that they are calling and any other information that has been uploaded with the file of phone numbers (on campaigns that's typically name, age, party registration, and where they live). This means instead of talking to three or four people an hour, you can talk to upwards of twenty-five people per hour. With a dialer it should take four thousand to five thousand hours of calling to talk to one hundred thousand voters. Much easier than twenty-five thousand hours!

In the field offices where paid staff were directly managing volunteers, they were using the dialer that came with the voter file software. But there was no way we could have given unsupervised volunteers access to the Iowa state VAN dialer that was managed out of the local offices. It would have been too expensive, the permissions were too complicated to give out to hundreds of thousands of people from out of state, and it would have potentially disrupted the state operation.

What's more, in 2015, the FCC issued new rules under the Telephone Consumer Protection Act (TCPA) that meant you couldn't use predictive dialers like the one that came with VAN to call mobile numbers. You could only use them for landlines. We needed a web-based dialer that wasn't an auto-dialer for mobile numbers. Meaning each call had to be initiated by a human instead of a machine.

The campaign agreed we needed a dialer for the volunteer army we were building and was engaging with a virtual call center software company that largely sells its platform to debt collectors. How ironic. I'm not going to name the company here because I wouldn't recommend you use it. Negotiations were complete on a web-based dialer that would be TCPA compliant, but we had to wait for hundreds of little decisions to be made about its implementation on the campaign. It was confusing to use. Logging in was difficult.

The discussions around launching the web-based dialer in December got side-tracked into a project to build a custom layer of software on top of it: a Bernie-branded user interface that would have a common log-in with other campaign web properties.

Yes, the web dialer interface was truly terrible. Most companies don't care about how terrible the user experience is for someone working for minimum wage harassing people (who are most likely in debt) from an American call center or for even lower wage workers in an offshore operation in the Philippines. But I'd been involved in custom software development before. And just the mention of a "unified log-in" project filled me with a soul-crushing sense of doom. Even if they thought this could be done in a few weeks, it would take Saikat Chakrabarti away from iterating on the tools that we were relying on to scale up the number of volunteers whom we would be depending on to use the dialer.

If we wanted to be ready to capture and channel all the of the energy we believed would be unleashed January 2, we needed this web-based dialer up and running in December so we could teach people how to use it, discover and squash bugs, and get the data flowing into VAN so that it could then be accessed by staff and volunteers on the ground to turn out the voters we needed to win. It was already months overdue—but we still had time to bring volunteer phone banking into the campaign in a way that might make a significant difference.

"Why can't we just try using it like it comes out of the box," I asked. I was told that the volunteers couldn't use it in its current state. I sort of agreed on one level. It was an awful tool. And they hadn't purchased access to a feature that would have allowed us to put the scripts in the tool itself, so they popped up on the screen along with the voter's name when a live call was connected to a volunteer. We would have this truly ugly calling interface, and the volunteers would also have to print out or keep open a Google doc with a script! But for a campaign organization that was struggling with very basic tasks—like getting the VAN and targeting up and running outside of the first four states—doing custom software development wasn't that much more attractive in my experience. So many problems could come up. Development could be late. It could be buggy if they didn't test it well enough. There could be data handoff issues. Would the APIs be sluggish and thus make page loads slow? It could be late and still be bad. It could be a nightmare.

After this was discussed on a conference call, I got Saikat, whom I was just getting to know, on the phone. I was probably overly impressed by his credentials as an early employee at Stripe. I also felt slightly awkward at having argued against having him build an interface for the dialer during the meeting. To my relief Saikat said he agreed with my approach to just give the dialer to some volunteers and see what the barriers were. Maybe we could avoid a development project altogether. That meant a lot coming from someone who had built two products with millions of users behind them.

I went back to the data team and instead of trying to kill the whole project just said I would try the tool "as is" with some volunteers, and then we could provide feedback on what the big sticking points were. We only needed a way to generate log-ins which could be created using a Google form that fed into the software's API.

All this had transpired in the days immediately before the retreat. So after Claire announced the seemingly impossible goal of the one hundred thousand conversations before Iowa, I announced that the only way it would work is if we got the web-based dialer up and running.

With the exception of Sam Briggs, a staffer who had used web-based dialers extensively in the past, and Zack and Claire, whom I'd been haranguing about this for months, hardly anyone even knew what a dialer was.

We added time to the agenda to discuss the web-based dialer and devise a launch plan. But as we worked on the plan, someone said, "This is complicated and people will have to complete a webinar before they can make calls using this tool." Ceci went further: "We really need to make a training video." Corbin talked about the need to get in touch with all the hosts and walk them through this personally. There needed to be a detailed written guide as well. The list just got lengthier from there. The more we discussed it, the longer it was going to take to get to launch. It was already December 12. By the time we got ready to launch, it would be too close to Christmas and we'd have to wait until after that.

After whiteboarding all of the things that needed to happen to launch the dialer and realizing that this planning was going to take over our entire retreat, I suggested that what we needed was a deadline. "We're going to launch this dialer in three days, and the first people to test it will be the nurses in Oakland who had a phone bank planned for December 16."

People were not happy. How were we supposed to launch a major program in just a few days? As far as I was concerned, we needed a list of voters to call, a script in a public Google doc, and a one-pager on how to use the dialer. Thankfully, Ari Trujillo-Wesler had my back. She had been detailed to our team from the data department. She was suffering at the time from a terrible case of the flu, and so we were trying to lean on her sparingly (and avoid getting infected at such a key moment in the campaign!). But I knew she was, at her core, preternaturally biased toward action. "Ari, is it possible you could get us a universe of phone numbers set up in the dialer and make some log-ins?" "Yes!" she said, and she was on it.

In the weeks ahead, Ari would earn hero status on a daily basis as she constantly pushed toward action and more action, and patiently plowed through the chaos that was to come on the dialer project with drive, dedication, and indefatigable work ethic.

We were going to get this ugly system up in three days. There would be problems, but we already were having problems. Volunteers had been complaining about how few voters they were talking to for the hours they were putting in at the phones. And again, building out custom software on top of the dialer was also guaranteed to come with problems—just problems closer to the election!

If we were going to demonstrate that this could be done, people on the team were going to have to be motivated by more than my arbitrary deadline. It was time to eat some of our own dog food. We were going to have a phone bank right in that conference room.

Sam Briggs sprung into action to organize it. Sam was a veteran organizer that I pulled onto the campaign because we had worked together on CREDO SuperPAC. His first job in politics was as a field organizer for a MoveOn.org antiwar project in 2007 called Americans Against Escalation in Iraq. The idea of that project was to hold Republicans, who voted to authorize the Iraq war, accountable with bird dogging and protests. He worked on a series of local and state campaigns and eventually came to CREDO SuperPAC, where he had run a congressional independent expenditure campaign and later served as national field director.

Sam operates at about 2.7 times the speed of a normal human being. He has a high organizing metabolism. He is that guy who, when organizers complain that we are working volunteers too hard by having them phone bank for two whole hours straight, wants to know why they aren't being scheduled into three-hour shifts (an exchange that did indeed happen on our team). Sam is a true believer in volunteer-voter contact, and peer-to-peer organizing. It has something to do with growing up Jehovah's Witness in Tucson, Arizona. By the time Sam became an organizer, he had knocked on countless doors as part of the regular proselytizing he did with his congregation. He was used to so few people opening the door when they saw the Jehovah's Witnesses coming that, as far as Sam was concerned, his response rate when making phone calls or knocking on doors for candidates or issue advocacy campaigns was "amazing."

Sam decided that the best way to onboard the team to the dialer was first to have them make calls using the manual system. He wanted the staff on the distributed organizing team to get a visceral sense of what we were putting the volunteers through without access to a web-based dialer. It was painful. I knew this because I had hosted a phone bank in my home, just like we were asking volunteers to do. Three passionate Bernie volunteers came over to my apartment in San Francisco: a digital marketer, a college student, and an artist who has a piano that he puts on a truck bed and plays in various places around town. They were awesome, but it was brutal. I think I talked to five people in two hours. Not the best use of my time or of the volunteers' for that matter.

Under Sam's direction, distributed staff made calls using the manual system. Saikat and Claire were making calls for the first time. (Shamefully, Zack somehow ducked out, but he would attend his first volunteer phone bank a week later.) You'd be surprised how many people who run campaigns have never participated in the activities that they ask volunteers to spend their time on. Dialing each number individually, the staffers who had not yet joined the campaign's phone-banking efforts from the volunteer side had a bad feeling. They'd been hearing complaints from the volunteers that this was not an efficient use of their time. Now everybody on the team knew exactly what that felt like.

After the distributed staff spent a half hour dialing manually, Sam had everyone log into the web-based dialer. Ari played the role that volunteers would eventually play as live administrators clicking each number into a queue where it would be dialed by the system and then served up to the phone bankers who were logged in. It was slow at first. One call every five minutes. But then it started to pick up, and soon everyone was talking to voters on the phone. Soon there were only ten to fifteen second wait times before another voter popped up on the line.

So there we were, all sitting together in a seventeen-by-thirty-foot conference room on the top floor of the hotel. There were big windows looking out over Seattle skyline (remember, we got it for almost nothing thanks to the Berner day-shift manager!). We were talking with voters in South Carolina because it was easier for Ari to get us access to those numbers than Iowa or New Hampshire. Ceci had phone-banked more voters for Bernie than the rest of us put together. Corbin was also a natural on the phone.

But it was Sam who really stole the show, demonstrating his phone-banking virtuosity, which had been honed by all those years as a door-to-door child evangelist. As Saikat and Sam Ghazey, our intern from the University of Vermont, watched Sam take calls, their admiration grew into a full-blown organizer crush. They tried to pick up some of his best lines and imitate his demeanor. Sam's face was animated. He made electric connections with people in spite of the boilerplate campaign-approved script, which was pretty boring. Logged into the dialer, the calls started coming in rapid fire, and everyone saw how we could make the numbers fall into place. Also, phone banking just feet away from an insanely great pro like Sam

Briggs helped the team feel the raw power of the connections that can be made when engaging in peer-to-peer voter contact. After an hour of taking calls in the dialer, Saikat, Sam Ghazey, and the rest of the team were in. It didn't matter how terrible the tool was (and it was a pretty awful software user experience), going from talking to two people an hour to twenty people an hour was going to be awesome. We knew the volunteers were going to love this—and that their excitement would pull in wave after wave of new people.

As we shifted the retreat agenda to deal with the nuts and bolts of making this transition from manual calling to a dialer, it was clear the rollout was going to be rough. Staff would have to operate the software backend manually, clicking on every number in our universe to start the process of an efficient calling experience for volunteers. This would eventually be taken care of by volunteers, thanks to Ceci who set up a complicated management structure among hundreds of people with complete formal job descriptions, when we were calling and clicking on numbers for over a dozen states at once. The initial process was so rough, in fact, that I announced to the team that I was going to have to be at the launch in Oakland (where we had more than twenty volunteers coming in for the nurse-run phone bank) if we were going to keep our three-day schedule. We wouldn't have the training materials done, so I'd have to do it in person. I changed my flight to go to Oakland a day earlier, taking public transit straight from the airport directly to the nurse's office.

I knew it would be a rocky volunteer experience, and it was. Logging in was a nightmare, as we had to disable pop-up blockers on computers one by one. The interface had tiny type and was confusing. It wasn't clear how to enter into the database the outcome of each call. At first we couldn't get the dialer started, and then it was so successful we ran out of numbers halfway through the shift.

It wasn't perfect, but it had the makings of something big.

You may think, okay, I get the larger point, but why did you need to go on at such length about web-based dialers? Most people reading this book aren't going to be staff on a presidential campaign. But even if you aren't going to use a dialer, we wanted you to see how hard it was—and how scary it was—for us to go big instead of trying to be perfect.

Also, we think scaling person-to-person contact will be key to any kind of big organizing in the coming years. It's important for anyone who wants to do big organizing and scale meaningful engagement between people. To organize peer-to-peer contact via the phone at scale, dialers can help in almost any size campaign. If you're a lone activist, you can take a spreadsheet of city employees, put it in a dialer, and then whip through the whole list in a fraction of the time it would take to do it dialing one by one. You could even prerecord a message from yourself that could be left on voice-mails the dialer encounters while you're already on the next live call. Let's say you need members of the community to attend a local commission meeting on permits related to shipping fossil fuels through your town. You could get a voter file for your local area and then call through a list of voters living within five miles of passing oil trains and invite them to join you at the meeting. A dialer is also helpful for dividing up the work among multiple volunteers. Instead of dividing up a list of numbers and giving ten volunteers a spreadsheet of numbers to call, put all the numbers in a dialer and give those ten volunteers a log-in. You can control when they can call, see which calls have been made, find out how long the conversations were, and if two of your volunteers blow you off, the other eight will still be able to call the numbers you would have assigned to the no shows. And everyone can do the calling from wherever they are—at work, home, school, or a local cafe with Wi-Fi.

Also, over one hundred thousand of Bernie's best supporters were logged into the dialer at some point—and if you are one of them and were wondering why it was not more gracefully designed, now you know!

The lessons we learned on the campaign were sometimes counterintuitive but generally pretty simple. In fact, this rule in particular would be easier to implement anywhere *but* on a presidential campaign, where people tend to want you to go through eighteen levels of sign-off on everything that the public will see.

It was radical on a presidential campaign to simply use the virtual call center software solution marketed largely to debt collectors and not worry about having a slick interface on top with our brand and a unified log-in. We just shared our scripts in Google apps since we couldn't get them embedded in the software. This turned out to be better than fine, as when our scripts had mistakes in them, volunteers used the comment feature to send us suggested edits. We decided we'd put the dialer out there before training materials were complete and see if people could figure it out while we caught up with the necessary documentation. In the end we did come up with a one-page guide and we held optional webinars, but as it turned out, people didn't need nearly as much hand-holding as we thought. We launched in three days with something messy instead of waiting to launch something pretty with more features and a complete training package a month later.

This rule is even more important for smaller organizations and volunteer-led movements that want to be big than it was for a well-resourced presidential campaign. The fewer people you have in your organization or community group, the more work you need to put in the hands of volunteers. Get the work started and figure it out as you go along.

Learn the Basics
of Good Management

★ becky ★

G ood management is not counterrevolutionary. In fact, you need to master the art of management to give your revolution a fighting chance.

The work of social change is hard. And it can take a long time. People are passionate and there is so much at stake. It's easy to feel like whatever you are doing right now, however you are doing it, is the most important thing in the world. That might be fine if you're working all by yourself, but to do most big things you have to work on a team, and teams need a healthy management culture. Being part of a great team doing valuable work for an urgent cause is one of the most rewarding experiences any organizer can have.

In my career I've had the added perspective of spanning several worlds. I saw the world of telecom when I was an executive at CREDO Mobile. I witnessed management in the nonprofit world while running CREDO Action and as a board member of the once magnificent but eventually failed New Organizing Institute. And I saw political campaign management as president of CREDO Super-PAC, cofounder of the Secretary of State Project, and senior advisor on Bernie 2016. I can say hands down that I witnessed the worst management failings in Democratic electoral campaigns, followed by nonprofits, with the most consistent, respectful, and informed management in my corner of the corporate world.

Of course, there are also well-managed nonprofits and corporations that are terrible places to work. The point is that, just because you share a mission, it doesn't mean it's okay to throw the principles of good management out the window. And management isn't just about what people do in relation to the people reporting directly to them. It's about our mutual responsibility to create an environment where great work can get done, where people are respected while being held accountable, and where leaders use scarce resources wisely by making the best decisions possible while ensuring that crucial work gets done in a timely manner.

Revolutions are hard enough, so it's essential that members of a team don't make the work more difficult than it already is by behaving in ways that lead to inefficiencies, emotional exhaustion, and possible lawsuits! Revolutionary teams need to be hard-driving, results-oriented, nimble, respectful, and adaptive to constant change. Members of a team need to appreciate uncomfortable questions, welcome new strategies, and align quickly and move to implementation when a direction is set. We're in this to win. But we're also in this together. At the end of the day, you want to be able to love the other people who are on your team. To make this more likely, you need to learn the basics of good management.

Early in my time on the Bernie distributed organizing team I drafted a document for the team about "how we want to be," offering guidelines for creating an environment that encouraged good management. Here is a version of those principles. They are written specifically for people working on elections, but they could be adapted for any campaign or movement.

We will be outcome-focused.

Process is important, but we care most about outcomes. That means decisions are based on outcomes, not on personal concerns. We don't take things personally. We don't make things personal. We trust in the team to set the best course possible, and we all work in whatever way we're asked to by leadership in order to achieve our goals.

We will respect and learn from volunteers.

On our team, we make our impact through the massive amounts of work that volunteers are willing to do. All of our systems must be optimized for helping volunteers make the biggest possible impact. There are three ways that volunteers can make the biggest impact: (1) going door to door talking to voters; (2) talking to targeted voters on the phone; and (3) helping the campaign increase the number of volunteers engaged in (1) and (2). Some of the most productive volunteers can also be the most annoying at times. We will love and attend to the annoying ones, even when we don't want to. That said, if annoyance turns into real disruption and diminishes our capacity or other volunteers' capacity to produce voter contacts, we'll do what it takes to change the behavior of or fire disruptive volunteers.

We will practice "high input, low democracy" as a team.

Our team needs everyone at every level to bring suggestions to the table for making our work better. That means improving our volunteer engagement, bettering tool performance, and exceeding our voter contact goals. We won't win if everyone doesn't contribute the best ideas, offer constructive criticism when appropriate, engage in problem solving, and help anticipate future problems as we scale. That said, it's up to project leaders to make decisions and for the rest of the team to align with those decisions. Fast and effective decision making can't happen by consensus, but it should be informed by all the smart people we have working on the team across various areas of expertise.

We will choose speed over perfection.

A campaign happens on an accelerated time frame. There is a deadline, and we don't have the luxury of all the time we need to get things right. We will be more successful in exceeding our goals if we prioritize the fastest solution that is good enough over the perfect solution. That said, there are some errors we should never tolerate.

We will embrace productive conflict but not yelling.

Because we encourage passionate disagreement to make our organizing better, we need safeguards to ensure this doesn't escalate from productive to unproductive conflict. We never allow anyone to yell at or raise their voice with a member of our team. This includes team members, staff members in other departments, and even volunteers. Everyone at all levels has a responsibility to pause any interaction where there is yelling or someone perceives that they are being yelled at. If the conversation can be continued at least a half hour later with no yelling, fine. If not, escalate it to a manager.

We will not get into email trouble.

If there is disagreement in a Slack thread, quickly move to a real-time conversation on the phone or use the hangout feature to communicate face to face. It's easy for tone or intent to be misconstrued online. Don't send emails when you are upset. Take the time to work through your emotions, including reaching out to another team member, before responding (either in person or in writing).

We operate on East Coast time.

The campaign operates on East Coast time, and so does our team, unless you have a role that specifically requires you to keep alternate hours. No matter what coast we're on, we will all be available for core weekday business hours: 10:30–6:30 ET. If we cannot be available during core business hours on a given day, we'll make sure our manager is okay with that and we'll let the team know. Of course, all of us will be working extensively outside of these hours, but agreeing to be available during these will help us work together as a team across time zones.

We will not be defeated by meetings.

We will keep our daily team check-in to fifteen minutes most days. Other meetings should be scheduled on an as-needed basis and should be no more than fifty minutes, to allow people a brief break before their next meeting. No meeting should break the sixty-minute mark. If you still have more work to accomplish, schedule another meeting following a minimum thirty-minute break. Agendas and time limits can help meetings be more productive and encourage meeting participants to achieve desired outcomes in the time allotted.

We will eat our own dog food.

In order to design the best model for volunteer-voter contact, we need to be participating in our own programs. Everyone on the team should engage regularly in voter contact, using the tools promoted by the distributed organizing team. That can mean volunteering to call other volunteers via the Bernie Dialer tool, volunteering to host or attend phone banks, or following through on any call to action emphasized by the distributed organizing team. This is the best way to understand the volunteer experience and provides valuable feedback to our team. It is also respectful. It shows to the volunteers that we think what we are asking them to do is so valuable that we also make time to do it ourselves.

We will take care of ourselves and each other, and take necessary breaks without slowing down the work.

This is a marathon, not a sprint. Everybody needs to take necessary breaks (within reason and in coordination, so as not to inconvenience others). While we're all sacrificing our comfort and health to some degree to work on a campaign, it's important to remember that we're more productive soldiers for the revolution when we get a decent amount of sleep, eat regular meals, and get some basic exercise—even if it's just taking a twenty-minute walk during the day at some point. If you start skipping sleep, skipping meals, and not moving for days on end, your health and your work will both suffer. If you have such an intense workload that you feel like you don't have time to take care of yourself in a basic way on a continual basis, talk to your manager.

We will be grateful for our team.

This is an amazing team and a once-in-a-lifetime chance to help elect a president who will truly change things. When we hold each other and ourselves accountable, if we fall short of what this moment requires of us, we will do it with a spirit of forgiveness and generosity. We are grateful for this opportunity and recognize what an honor it is to work with each other and the volunteers to build the political revolution.

———————

If you're a manager of staff or volunteers, you'll also need to acknowledge that when hiring, you need to do thorough reference checks, especially if you think you know the applicant. You also need to give other people both positive and negative feedback, and ensure that your own time management idiosyncrasies don't make it hard for others to do their work on time.

Being willing to hold people accountable—especially on a campaign, where time and money are precious resources—is essential. This means being ready to fire people—both paid staff and volunteers. Firing someone is never easy. On campaigns there is often a tendency just to layer someone who was failing or, worse, to have them "fail up" and promote them to a less hands-on role. This dynamic is destructive in a couple of ways. First, it allows people who are ineffective to hold down a position that plenty of people out there would be better at and are dying to have. Second, it can be demoralizing to the people who are working hard, exceeding expectations, and deserve teammates who can deliver.

I was laid off in the big round of layoffs at the end of April 2016. There was a lot of criticism about that round of layoffs, but it was true that at that point in the primary calendar the campaign needed to downsize and reallocate cash. I supported the idea of layoffs at that scale and was absolutely okay to be among those getting the ax. In fact, I stayed in touch and continued to volunteer as I was able.

The revolution could definitely use more and better management! Changing the world is hard work. And when it's funded by small-dollar donations, it's important to make every little bit help. That means hiring and firing quickly when needed but also taking the time you need to do it right.

We can be tough competitors, highly accountable managers, and still be humane partners in our shared struggle. No matter what your role is, as a staffer or volunteer, seek mentors and other resources to help make you a better manager and a better member of your team. Reading the book *Managing to Change the World* is one place to start.

If There Are No Nurses, I Don't Want to Be Part of Your Revolution

★ becky ★

N ursing as a profession is based on the values of caring, compassion, and community, and nurses are powerful allies who will attract countless others to your cause. They possess a down-to-earth professionalism that is sincere and authentic, and they have firsthand knowledge of the life-or-death stakes of the most urgent issues of the day, from income inequality to immigration reform to climate change.

I'm serious when I say that if there are no nurses, I don't want to be part of your revolution.

In poll after poll, nursing is named by Americans as the most-trusted profession. No other profession is even close. Meanwhile, there's a four-way tie for the least-trusted professions: lobbyists, members of Congress, telemarketers, and car salespeople.

When National Nurses United endorsed Bernie Sanders for president (they were the first national union to do so), NNU president RoseAnn DeMoro said "Bernie's issues align with nurses from top to bottom." The same could be said about a true political revolution by the people. Not only do nurses' issues align with a revolutionary agenda, but nurses make amazing revolutionary leaders.

You can think of nurses as the indicator species for real revolution. Nursing as a profession is based on the values of caring, compassion, and community. It's not just health care policy that they concern themselves with. In her endorsement, DeMoro explained that nurses "have to care for the fallout of every social and economic problem—malnutrition, homelessness, unpayable medical bills, the stress and mental disorders from joblessness, higher asthma rates, cancer, heart ailments, and birth defects from environmental pollution and the climate crisis. Bernie Sanders's prescriptions best represent the humanity and the values nurses embrace."

Social media and the mainstream media elite fueled the misconception that the driving force behind the Bernie campaign was so-called "Bernie bros": white, male, and aggressively antifeminist. But those of us who experienced the campaign in real life as opposed to on television or Facebook knew that the Bernie campaign's grassroots was led by nurses and a lot of people who were like them: a diverse group of working and middle class people, the majority of whom were women.

The nurses had big red buses, and they volunteered with their trademark red scrubs. The buses were in constant rotation in states from New Hampshire to New York State, from Colorado to California. Sometimes Ben Cohen of Ben & Jerry's would come off the bus, and there would be an ice cream party while the nurses registered voters. Other times they stormed a campaign office and went out to canvas en masse.

National Nurses United happens to be headquartered in Oakland, California, and it was one of my first stops when I joined the Bernie campaign. At CREDO SuperPAC our best volunteers in our Sacramento area office had been members of the California Nurses Association, who often stopped by after their shift was over to call voters in our successful effort to defeat Republican Congressman Dan Lungren in 2012. I knew that when it came to work around elections, not only could nurses get things done, but they were also the best people to spend time with.

I met with Holly Miller, who is the national director of public advocacy for NNU, and it was the shortest meeting ever. She said straight away, "Tell us what we can do to help and we'll be there." It was such a welcome contrast to our many other allies who, with the best of intentions, attached all kinds of conditions and quid pro quos to their offers of assistance. I left the meeting thinking I needed to figure out what to ask for and that I probably should make it something big.

A few weeks later I had an idea. We were about to launch a virtual call center that would be far more complicated but vastly more powerful than having volunteers dial voters one by one. (This system is described in "Rule 11: Don't Let the Perfect Be the Enemy of the Big.") It would make our volunteers many times more effective. But the software interface was terrible. Even the log-in process was not easy.

The National Nurses United office was located in a big building just a block from a major BART transit stop in Oakland. They had big meeting rooms on the first floor—which happened to have multiple phone lines in them to support the union's organizing activities. What if we tested our new dialer on volunteers at the nurses' headquarters, and we had some nurse volunteers to coach people along and get them to work on a tool we knew would be frustrating and probably plagued with bugs in the beginning?

I asked Holly, and she instantly set me up with nurse volunteers who could help make this happen. They became our beta-testing lab and allowed us to get our Bernie dialer up and running weeks earlier than would have been possible otherwise.

Once all the primaries and caucuses were over, the nurses convened a People's Summit in Chicago that gathered Bernie volunteer leaders and some of the best Bernie surrogate spokespeople. The genius of the meeting was having it at the end of their annual membership conference for nurses. Before I knew that this was their plan, I'll admit to being a little skeptical—wondering if the weekend would be yet another gathering of all the usual suspects. But the huge crowd that gathered at the Chicago convention center was amazing and filled with nurses. It's impossible to adequately describe the difference that this made.

At every barnstorm and phone bank meeting we attended, we found that the dominant demographic was women who had working class jobs, service jobs, and professional jobs such as health care worker or teacher. Their sincerity and authenticity, their concern for everyone, their down-to-earth professionalism, and their firsthand understanding of the life-or-death stakes of the campaign for millions of Americans helped make Bernie's movement great. If you've got nurses in your revolution, you know at least you've got a shot.

Grow Complexity by Solving Problems as They Arise

★ zack ★

In a successful movement, campaign, or revolution, everything is growing and changing too fast to make detailed long-term plans. Nevertheless, to grow big, processes will have to become more and more complex. Grow complexity by solving practical problems as they arise in conversation with involved leaders.

By telling—not asking—our team that we were launching the dialer by a deadline that was a few days away, Becky opened a Pandora's box.

As she left our Seattle summit early to launch the first phone bank to be powered by the new dialer, she unleashed a world of chaos, but with it came the hope that we could build something huge by bringing order to the chaos. It would all depend on whether a few people on our staff and a handful of key super volunteers, with support from the data team, could continue to assemble and adapt volunteer teams to the task of running the biggest virtual call center ever built for a presidential primary.

Over the next month, we constructed a complex system of interdependent volunteer teams that managed not only the dialer tool and the data inflows and outflows but also supported the phone bank events (sometimes thousands of them per week), the barnstorms that produced them, and also phone bankers who just wanted to call from home on their own. We did not sit down in the beginning of it all and decide on a giant structure—though there were moments when some of us were tempted to do so! The reason we were able to build a working structure successfully in such a short time was that the teams added roles, processes, and other forms of complexity as solutions in response to real problems.

There were hundreds of thousands of people who wanted a way to help Bernie but were nowhere near any campaign office or staff. We finally had a way they could do something valuable—and with the dialer, we believed it would also be satisfying. I'd made calls on the dialer and was convinced that it was going to suck everyone in and be amazing—the only question was whether we could pull the process together in a way that scaled and actually worked.

Our task revolved around a dialer product used by professional call centers that allows dialing cell phones legally—the dialer product the field offices were using only allowed dialing to landlines. (This system is described in "Rule 11: Don't Let the Perfect Be the Enemy of the Big.") Our dialer product is legal because each call is actually manually initiated by a person. By dividing the work of dialing and talking, the dialer made it possible to get almost the same number of people on the line as we would have with a true "predictive dialer."

After our meeting in Seattle, Ari began to load the data into the dialer each day for the few states that were ready for us to call. Ceci provided new webinars to train users on the new system several times a day. Sam Briggs, Ceci, and Ari handled the tasks of initiating each call by clicking on a phone number to start its journey through the dialer system and of resolving issues relating to data, user accounts, and so on. For the states we were allowed to call into, Becky drafted customized guides that she had whipped up on her flight to the nurses' phone bank in Oakland, our test site.

Phone-banking enthusiasts who were used to visiting our phone-banking site each day were now offered something new: the Bernie Dialer—with a promise that they were going to love it.

And they did love it! Soon, there were so many users that Sam, Ceci, and Ari were becoming overwhelmed. Ceci brought in two volunteers named Kyle Machado and Cole Edwards to help, knowing that they were probably going to become our interns in Burlington and hoping that they would be able to help drive the system as it grew.

Very quickly, though, this small team was totally overloaded. As a key member of our tiny data team, Ari had a lot of other things to do in the day besides click on phone numbers. As more and more people logged in to make calls each day, the mountain of numbers to click grew taller and taller.

According to Kyle, "It was horrifying. The numbers would stack up. They were like giant walls. It was almost like Tetris in reverse. As you clicked, the tiles with the phone numbers disappeared. If there were a lot of callers and not enough clickers, everything stacked up and backed up. You'd be clicking as fast as you could, but you'd see the scroll bar shrinking down and down," which meant an unseen mountain of unclicked numbers were piling up below the screen— voters that could be reached if only you had more clickers!

No problem. Everyone knew what to do next: form a new volunteer team. This pattern had been established in the DNA of our department.

Sam took the lead in kick-starting the dialer monitor team (they decided "clickers" sounded too unglamorous). But Sam was way too busy with a million other things, including supporting the burgeoning state field and communications teams in states all over the country. So Sam gave the job of forming the team to Kyle, who had officially joined our staff as a paid intern just days earlier.

"I remember Sam created a PowerPoint presentation for recruiting volunteers for the team on webinars," Kyle recalled at one point. "I had never looked at the PowerPoint because I got it right before the first training call. I was on a call with fifty volunteers, and I had never done anything like this before in my life. I was thrown to the wolves! This is just how it played out. I was literally reading the PowerPoint for the first time as I was on the webinar. It didn't go well, but the volunteers learned what they needed. And ten of the fifty people on that call are still involved now."

I'm going to give you just a few examples of the crises, decision points, and solutions that the team faced as time went on that allowed them to succeed and drive the program past seventy-five million calls by the time the campaign was done.

These are real problems that arose as the program scaled. These problems, not abstract notions or grand visions, became the triggers for the decisions that led to adding new teams, new roles, new procedures, and new levels of complexity.

To address the problem of too many callers, not enough clickers, the new dialer monitor team was brought onto Slack, where Kyle, Ceci, Sam, and Ari gave the members instructions and kept the action happening. When there were too many clickers and not enough callers, they would tell some clickers to switch to the phones. When the situation was reversed, they would get on Slack and ask for clickers.

Meanwhile, word of the Bernie Dialer was spreading across Facebook and Reddit from Bernie volunteer to Bernie volunteer. Everyone was buzzing that there was finally a way to be a productive voter contact worker from wherever you lived. Not only were volunteers chomping at the bit to get started but so were the handful of state field programs that were getting up and running.

We tried to make a plan to roll out the Bernie Dialer to one state at a time. But then Ari—who had an admirable predisposition toward action and an equally laudable state field organizer's allegiance to the staff on the ground—started turning on the dialer for all the staffed states. Ari, who was in the data team but assigned to work with us, was an instinctive team builder and a fantastic trainer, and she trusted volunteers to do hard and sophisticated work. Ari had been a state data staffer on the Obama campaign in 2008. I was so excited to have her on the campaign and on our side. I knew she would be an amazing asset and she was.

With virtually all the staffed states coming online at the same time, everything began exploding. It was hectic as hell. There were too many people in the dialer monitors' Slack channel to manage—and too much monitoring to take care of with a random assortment of whoever showed up. Schedules were needed. Plans. Discipline.

And this—the team decided—called for a new role: monitor coordinators!

Ceci, Sam, and Kyle invited the "cream of the crop" of the dialer monitors to join the new team. They invited people who had basic leadership instincts and "who weren't disruptive or weird," people who were clearly trying to help others. Then—as usual—there was an invitation to a call, a conference call to train for the new role, and invitations to a new Slack channel. And off they went!

Everything got more formal at this point. Dialer monitors (DMs) and monitor coordinators (MCs) signed up for scheduled shifts. And with a gradually rotating group of super volunteers, a few staff people—also rotating over time—spent hours and hours on conference calls identifying and solving large and small problems with the system as it grew.

"Conference calls. All day every day. We hashed out everything," Hannah recalls.

"And we had conference calls about the conference calls. I could have done without those," Cole remembers.

Becky was a little horrified when she learned how much time the teams spent on conference calls, but it was important that we erred on the side of getting the details right, even if it meant spending a huge amount of time on the phone. After all, even though the staff never stopped "eating their own dog food" and kept doing frontline work, the volunteer teams did the bulk of that work. It was the staff's responsibility to make sure that the details of this growing machine were working. And looking back, it's easy to see how a few unilateral decisions that were made without hashing out the details on a conference call didn't solve problems; they created them.

But mostly we addressed the problems and often figured out simple but consequential solutions. For example, initially, the shifts for DMs and MCs changed on the hour. DM shifts were one hour. MC shifts were two hours. Every two hours, therefore, there was a disruption when for a time there were no clickers and no managers, which meant that thousands of callers would be left stranded. Sam, Ceci, and Kyle learned about this problem because they held conference calls regularly with the volunteers who were doing the work.

Someone suggested a simple solution: change the MC shift on the half hour. Problem solved!

Scores of little problems like this were constantly worked out on calls and then implemented by volunteers on the Bernie campaign. But if this constant improvement isn't done with consistency, patience, and attention to detail, then it will all fall apart. You need to find the right personalities to drive that process: people who are detail-oriented, tenacious, and willing to stay in the weeds until they get things right.

At this point in the campaign, the technologies of the Bernie Dialer and the barnstorm—with all the teams that supported each— were feeding into each other and causing our numbers to spiral out of control. Everyone was burnt out. But they felt that what they were doing could be making a difference in the election, and they saw so many opportunities every day to grow our numbers and to improve the quality of the calls—so they kept on moving, kept on pushing, and kept on making everything better every chance they got.

After a string of successful barnstorms that Ceci and I did together all around Los Angeles, a volunteer leader named Dionne Charlotte realized that some of the people who signed up to be phone bank hosts never saw their events appear on the Bernie map.

"I know, Dionne, it's terrible. But some of the sheets are illegible. And there's little we can do about it," I said. We had tried to check the sheets at the events but many of the hosts were already gone by the time we had their sheets in hand.

Dionne had already been calling the phone numbers on the illegible sheets from the barnstorms she attended. She sussed out the info she needed and, as a member of the data entry team, created the events. But as one person, she was only able to do so many. She suggested we create a team.

At the same time, another volunteer, Elijah Browning, was pushing for us to form a team to call past phone bank hosts to ask them to repeat their events. We all thought Elijah was a New Yorker because he had been so involved in a campaign to convince New Yorkers to change their voter registrations before the ridiculously early deadline. Elijah, as it turned out, was a massage therapist who lived in Grand Rapids, Michigan, who was going broke as he took fewer and fewer clients to make more and more time for Bernie. It was working people like Elijah who made the Bernie campaign what it was: people giving up their own livings, even when they could not afford to do so, to do whatever they could for the revolution. They did it because they are the best people in the world. They understood that if some of us didn't fight back, that the whole world was doomed—and they fought even when it was counter to their own self-interest to do so.

Ceci put Dionne and Elijah together into a new team where their ideas quickly morphed into the plan to start by simply calling all hosts before their event—to answer questions, to encourage them to do turn out for their phone bank, and to make sure that they understood how to use the dialer and weren't still doing inefficient manual calling.

This was how we got the event-scheduling and maintenance (ESM) team—a team that would soon turn into a powerhouse of the calling operation. Ceci and Elijah quickly realized that this team was going to have a huge impact on the success of all phone banks. Soon, at every barnstorm we were meeting proud members of the ESM team. It was great having them at barnstorms because they could stand up and tell people what a great experience others were having with their phone bank parties.

I saw firsthand how badly we needed the ESM team while attending my first volunteer-led phone bank at the Overland Park, Kansas, public library. Some quirks of the dialer were preventing up to half of our phone bankers from making calls at all.

The ESM team began to communicate—among many other things—three crucial rules for the dialer. (1) Turn off the pop-up blocker that's on by default in most browsers. Without this turned off, the dialer wouldn't work. (2) Say "hello" to the voter right when you hear the beep. And (3) Click on "ready"!

As Becky has already explained, the user interface of the dialer was terrible. People didn't realize they needed to click a "ready" button to get started calling. At one early point, Ceci estimated that 20 percent of the people who logged into the dialer never hit "ready."

Administrators on the dialer could send a message to the caller: "Click the ready button!" But the interface was so bad that the caller was not likely to see it. Before the ESM team began reaching all hosts with the three rules of the dialer, admins would log out users who hadn't clicked "ready," in hopes that the change would make them notice the "ready" button when they logged back in.

There was so much room for improvement, if only our phone bank hosts could be prepared, which is exactly what the ESM team started doing.

What we found over and over was that once a team had a clear mission, it would chase that mission fanatically. Because of our rampant barnstorms crisscrossing the country, our numbers of phone-banking parties were exploding. The ESM team's mission was to talk to *every* host. At first this was a pipe dream, but they were going for it anyway. I remember talking to Ceci when they were calling only a fraction of hosts whose events were happening the next day. She set a goal to have the steady state be that the team would be calling hosts whose events were scheduled a week out. It took a little while, but she got there. And she got there by adding more and more people to the team and by working out processes that allowed them to do their job efficiently.

It got very, very difficult sometimes. To run the ESM team, someone had to download all the events that had been created the previous day, put them into a spreadsheet, and organize them so that the team, who had access to the sheet, could make and note their calls.

At first, that *someone* was a sixteen-year-old named Liam Clive who lived in Hawaii. His mother was from Kentucky and his father was from New Zealand—Hawaii was the compromise location. Not bad! Liam was good with Google spreadsheets, and he kept up as best he could. But soon it spun out of control. It's not possible to quickly explain why and how it got so messy in that spreadsheet. But it's an important part of this story, so you'll just have to trust me that it got crazy complex and unmanageable for unavoidable reasons. In the beginning, there were often hundreds of events pouring into the sheet each day. As more and more people joined the team and gained access to the sheet, more mishaps started to take place. Once, a troll got in there and started messing everything up on purpose. But even without intentional sabotage, well-meaning team members sometimes screwed everything up in the sheet.

Members of the team would call as many new events as possible—and mark them as contacted. But then everything needed to be sorted and hundreds of rows of data need to be moved around. It all came down to hundreds of little procedural and technical details. Just imagine, as they tried to sort out these problems, how complicated the discussions on their conference calls became!

Eventually, Ceci threw up her hands and said, "I give up!" Her solution: Microsoft. Remember, before joining us, Ceci had been leading projects at Washington Mutual for years. Over those years, there had been IT managers who had hooked up solutions for her to solve problems just like this. What she didn't remember was that the solutions took several years to implement—usually years that she was spared, as she was using the finished system. And, unfortunately, she remembered that Microsoft was involved.

Somehow a gaggle of progressive Microsoft employees got to Ceci and said they wanted to help, although it seemed unlikely we'd get them to roll up their sleeves and work in the spreadsheets of their corporate rival, Google.

When Ceci called me about this days before the Nevada caucus, I said, "No!"

She begged.

I said, "No!" and "Trust me!" about twenty times in that conversation.

By the end, she said, "Okay," defeated.

I told her I'd find her someone who could help. The thing was, I'd seen hundreds of attempts to fix problems like this through big, consultant-driven custom software processes. They always took a year or more and cost hundreds of thousands of dollars—when all that was needed was a few lines of well-placed code to hack a quick-and-dirty solution into place.

I went to Coders for Sanders—a Slack team that regrettably doesn't have the chapter it deserves in this book—and I wrote out a description of the problem Ceci faced and the kind of person we needed for a solution: "We need someone who is a real coder, but who will get down and dirty with a Google spreadsheet, who will listen to the users of this sheet and figure out a solution."

This is the kind of request that almost always goes unfulfilled. It was a Hail Mary. But lo and behold, the right person showed up. He was a guy named Mike Feher, a twenty-nine-year-old tech retiree in Lafayette, Louisiana, who, according to the team, had a "hippy Louisiana accent."

Mike emailed me after my post in Coders for Sanders:

Hey, I'm good to go and could write the api integration and help with data entry just let me know - mike

I was so busy at the time that I just sent this email back to him, CCing Liam, and never thought about it again:

OK great! But will you start by doing the tedious work each day so that you really understand what's going on and what's needed? That's what we need right now.

You need to be prepared to spend 1–3 hours per day just getting this data right each day.

What do you think? Please reply all and work it out with Liam.

Mike swooped in, got to work with Liam, listened, and fixed everything. Google sheets are actually codable. A sharp software developer can make magic happen in a spreadsheet. All kinds of data can fly around and reorganize itself in relation to each other and to instructions and parameters you give it. Mike saved the day, and suddenly Liam and Cole and others no longer needed to stay up until 3 a.m. just to keep things working—and better yet, the team was no longer slowed down by Google spreadsheet obstacles and was able to power ahead to achieve its goal of calling and preparing every phone bank host a week or more in advance.

It made a huge difference that phone bank hosts were being prepared in advance by the ESM team. But there were still so many potential phone calls that were being left on the table—so many phone bankers who *still* couldn't get started.

Remember, I'm leaving out scores of serious problems that were slowing things down and making life difficult for everyone at all levels. All of these problems had to be worked through on long conference calls by staff and volunteers—and sometimes vendors—scattered across time zones.

The team solved these problems as they came up. They didn't have a grand blueprint for what this was going to look like in the end. But they did look ahead to try to sort out the implications of potential solutions to problems. As complexity increases, getting the details right becomes more important. It takes time and patience.

When the team neglected to think through the implications of decisions a few steps into the future, there was peril. There was, for example, an issue with log-in accounts. The dialer product we were using was intended for call centers with a maximum of hundreds of employee users—not for thousands of volunteer users. The product had an arbitrary limit on the number of user accounts we could have live at any one time. We didn't fully think through the best way to solve this problem. Trying to avoid a few hours of hard discussions up front led to dozens of hours of even more painful conversations and tedious work down the line.

Just when we had taught everyone through the ESM team to "disable your pop-up blocker, click ready, and say hello at the beep," we began to have trouble with bad log-ins. The problem was that callers' user IDs and passwords kept changing or being deleted. It was hurting our growth.

We needed a live communication channel to ensure people could get logged in no matter what we had broken. Ceci consulted Craig Grella. She was thinking maybe an 800 number that we'd staff with volunteers, but Craig suggested a live chat tool—the kind that's appearing on so many websites to provide customer service. Live chat has the advantage of allowing an agent to carry on several conversations at one time. And for us it was perfect because 90 percent or more of the issues could be handled with a canned response such as, "We're so sorry, your password had to be changed. Please go here to reset it. . . ."

Hannah took the lead in forming the new team. She grew it using exactly the same process all the other teams used: She began by doing the work herself. Then she trained some volunteers. When the team grew to the point of becoming unwieldy, she created roles and gave volunteers responsibility and, with that responsibility, titles. The live chat team soon had live chat volunteers (LCVs) and point of contacts (PCs). I remember meeting some of Hannah's volunteers at a barnstorm.

"I'm a PC!" one said. I was proud that I didn't know what in the world she was talking about. It meant that a real organization was being built far beyond what a few of us had gotten started.

Sometimes the titles and team names that the teams created for themselves got a bit wonky and impenetrable, but what counted was that they stuck, they worked, and the volunteers were running it.

With all these teams, the phone-banking operation only got better and better.

Long after many people had given up on the Bernie campaign, volunteers were still plugging away, calling into the later states like New York, New Jersey, Connecticut, and, of course, California. Sam Briggs, working closely with Kyle, continuously fine-tuned the dialer, making it massively more efficient per caller. Paul Schaffer, who was on the data team, built an impressive dashboard that monitored every aspect of the program in real time. The final state of the phone-banking machine was awesome. If we had made it to the general election, we would have had the time to scale it to a ridiculous level, while also continuously working to improve call quality. It would have been amazing.

With a lot more lead time and a little more resources, our calling operation could have been much larger and massively more effective. This is one of the most important things for the manager of the next insurgent presidential campaign to learn about: Your campaign will have a virtually unlimited pool of volunteers who want to help you win. But it takes several months of painstaking work to build a system that works at scale. When you build it, don't buy some consultant's giant plan. Build it with the people and volunteers and technology that are available to you, and build it iteratively in steps by adding complexity only by solving problems as they arise.

Only Hire Staff Who Embrace the Rule "The Revolution Will Not Be Staffed"

★ zack ★

When you're lucky enough to staff up, make sure you don't hire anyone who will undervalue, patronize, or otherwise alienate and drive away volunteer leaders who are doing all the work. And if you find you have hired someone like that, fire them as soon as you can.

By late November 2015, we had a very large and growing volunteer infrastructure gearing up to pull off the national phone bank of the century. We were holding thousands of other kinds of events every month and were attempting to build a coherent organizing model that could do more on the ground than just phone bank in the forty-odd later states. All supported by just seven full-time staff.

It worked because the staff we had hired embraced the central role of volunteers. Some of them even had started as volunteers. They all understood that volunteers were our colleagues who were going to have to do the majority of the work of the campaign in the later states—not just repetitive work like making calls, but the complex management work of creating the systems to build and drive the phone banking machine and hopefully also all the other operations we had planned.

After Rich Pelletier joined the campaign as national field director in late November, we knew that many of the Super Tuesday and later states were going to get staffed. Before this, only Texas and Arkansas were staffed. Thanks to Rich, we were given the order to hire ten more people to support the digital organizing and email needs of the states that would be getting field staff.

My first thought was, "They're going to ruin it." Except for Becky and Claire, I'd sought to hire primarily super volunteers. I was worried that with this new mandate to hire staff, we'd get professionals coming in from traditional organizations who would not want (or know how) to work alongside volunteers as colleagues. In my head, I could already hear the calls that would come in from volunteers quitting after being patronized and sidelined by staff. And I could already hear staff dismissing volunteers every time one missed a deadline or got something wrong (as if staff never do those things).

And then something totally unexpected happened: Becky pulled, out of nowhere, a whole gaggle of incredibly talented, creative, experimental people who embraced that the revolution will not be staffed! It was as if Becky had been carrying them in her sleeve, waiting for the moment that we were given hiring slots.

Normally, I would have been worrying about how all these staff were going to be managed well. But I had known Becky long enough and had seen her in action on enough CREDO projects to realize that wouldn't be a problem. She's one of those incredible people in progressive politics who is not only a visionary and big thinker but also an excellent manager. Visionaries on the left are a dime a dozen, but visionaries who know how to hire and manage are rare. Becky is one of the very few people I know where both those qualities have miraculously manifested in the same person. Having her on board leads to visions that can actually be executed.

This was one of the great ways that Becky helped me before and after she joined the campaign: She shot down a lot of my schemes that were never going to work or that we just didn't have the resources for yet. But unusually for such a practical person, she also had no fear of embracing big crazy plans that we just might be able to implement— and she had the experience and instincts to pull them off.

After I first met Becky on a radio show in 2000, during which she deconstructed my bad strategy to save an election, I wondered why she kept reaching out to me. Every couple of years I would find myself in a taco place in San Francisco, where Becky has lived since graduating from college in 1992, dutifully giving updates about what I'd been doing and my latest wacky plans for projects that only rarely ever happened. As I was chaotically jumping from thing to thing, Becky was staying put at Working Assets/CREDO learning how to make big visions come true by managing, planning, hiring, and firing. Once she was on the Bernie campaign—bringing in an amazing team of people she had worked with or watched in action over the years, giving them clear roles, and managing them toward clear objectives—it all felt a bit providential.

I think that part of the reason typical political staffers don't often work as colleagues alongside volunteers is that the typical progressive staff culture is often close to a monoculture of a very particular subculture. Volunteers in the progressive movement, on the other hand, come from all different cultures and classes. Progressive staff culture, especially in national organizations, tends to be dominated by upper middle class white college graduates—and if that's not specific enough, they also tend to have assimilated into a specific urban subculture of highly educated, nonreligious people who even share specific similar habits and thinking around everything from food to exercise to child rearing. This is what makes the typical staff retreat for any progressive organization so awkward for someone from outside of this narrow subculture.

Another unusual thing about Becky, which was also true of the staffers she brought on board, was that even though she (like me) had gone off and assimilated into the progressive culture, she never forgot that it is indeed a subculture, and she never stopped treating people outside that culture as though they were, well, people, too. Becky grew up in Nashville, Tennessee, the buckle of the Bible Belt, where she attended church and had a great time with her youth group and at Vacation Bible School, even though she knew on some unconscious level she was going to have to leave and, in fact, did move to San Francisco after she came out in college. Now that I have emigrated to the Bible Belt (from suburban Connecticut!), Becky is one of the few progressives I can never impress with stories of my adopted "exotic" community.

The people Becky brought on board all just fit right in—and a big reason why each one of them came on board was that they believed in, and were excited by, the volunteer operation we were building.

Sam Briggs came from CREDO SuperPAC and before that MoveOn.org and many other movement jobs. Jon Warnow cofounded 350.org with a bunch of his classmates and their college professor, Bill McKibben, and had spent his entire career in politics empowering volunteers. Becky actually got Jon on the phone while he was in Paris for the signing of the historic climate accords and convinced him to leave his glamorous job and glorious tiny house in the San Francisco Bay Area for a desk in a tiny office in Burlington. Lilia Villa was a techie consultant and climate activist who shut down her own business and postponed her wedding to jump on the trail for Bernie. In the past she'd done a lot of relevant jobs, including training and technical customer support for a low-cost software platform that small community groups and down-ballot candidates use to run their campaigns. Will Easton was an email expert, but he came from CREDO Mobile where he had to be extremely customer-focused including jumping in to take sales calls. Daniel Souweine, a cofounder of Citizen Engagement Lab, was probably the furthest from the grassroots, but he was an excellent manager and Becky knew he would take on any task, adjust to any approach if it meant getting Bernie elected. And finally there was Zack Malitz, who cut his teeth in the early days of the antifracking movement (when it was practically all volunteer) and who had been working for Becky closely for three years at CREDO before jumping to the Bernie campaign shortly after she did.

There's no one formula to explain why the pros that Becky brought on board embraced that the revolution will not be, primarily, staffed. What's important is that she only hired people who did!

A little later, we had a second opportunity to add new staffers—critically, coming out of someone else's budget. There was a call for interns at headquarters that somehow we heard about, and someone at least once had told us that we would get some of these interns for our team. We assumed that these interns could come from anywhere, so I alerted the most impressive student organizers I knew who were eager to play a bigger role on the campaign. As it turned out, the people running the intern program were thinking that they'd just pick up a handful of University of Vermont students from the career center. But we pressed hard to get these firebrand students in, and they were accepted.

The five interns who joined our team in late December were Hannah Fertig from the University of Colorado Boulder and a tight-knit group of student organizers from a couple of community colleges in Orange County, California. The Orange County crew—Cole Edwards, Lynn Hua, Kyle Machado, and Alexandra Rojas—drove across the country to Burlington together on an epic barnstorming road trip.

It was natural for these new paid interns to work well with volunteers, of course, because they had been volunteers. They had been serving in major roles on the campaign locally, and most of them had been already getting sucked up into the snowball of sophisticated volunteer teams that Ceci and Sam were creating before they came on board as national campaign hires.

Getting the interns and the staff Becky recruited on board made a huge difference. But I remember worrying that, though we had more than doubled our staff, these paid organizers—who would be working fourteen hours a day, seven days a week—would just try to do everything themselves on whatever part of the campaign they were touching and would be crowding out volunteers. The problem with that wouldn't be one of principle but of practicality and scalability: If we cut the volunteers out of important roles simply because staff could handle a lot more, we'd never be able to add the volunteers back in. I feared that as we staffed up, the people working for the official campaign would demand more staff positions instead of adding more volunteer teams to scale the work. I also believed that after these five interns were onboarded we would never be allowed another staff position for the rest of the campaign—and I was right.

But the interns and the new staffers we hired never stopped bringing more and more volunteers into the fold. They never stopped seeing their jobs as unleashing the thousands of volunteers who wanted to do whatever they could to elect Bernie. In fact, those who had been volunteers before they joined the campaign felt an especially acute sense of urgency to give volunteers what they needed to get to work. This flowed from their own experience on the ground of being frustrated by the lack of direction that dominated before we got the dialer running, and from the endemic lack of literature, schwag, funds for renting event venues, and other resources local volunteer groups really needed.

When you get down to it, the heart of this rule is Rule 3—the revolution will not be staffed—but we still have to acknowledge that most movements need *some* people to be paid at some point. To achieve a certain scale, a nucleus of full-time, "locked-in" people are required, which usually means you have to hire some of them. When that happens, you want to make sure they don't kill the volunteer momentum that their role is meant to help grow. At its peak, the calling, texting, and other programs of the Bernie campaign were powered by probably hundreds of people who were putting in full-time or near full-time volunteer hours, many of whom played critical management roles in their organizations within the campaign. But the rule that "the revolution will not be staffed" isn't a purist command. It's a description of the reality of revolutionary movements.

Best Practices Become Worst Practices

★ zack ★

As conditions change, what used to be "best practices" can become counterproductive distractions. Don't enshrine "best practices." Continually reevaluate best practices not just to improve on them but so you can throw them out when a counterintuitive approach proves to be far more valuable.

It was our biggest barnstorm weekend ever: nine events in New York City in the space of two days during mid-January 2016. We were all exhausted. I was at a large Brooklyn beer garden with half of the distributed organizing team where soon we'd be having an epic barnstorm meeting. Staff were frantically getting all of our materials ready as the large venue filled up to standing room only. One big problem emerged: The microphone barely reached to a spot that would allow the room to see the speaker. Awkward, but the show had to go on.

As I was stuffing our leftover materials under a table, a man in his late eighties with a Brooklyn accent thicker than Bernie's started berating me for "screwing up the whole meeting"—and it hadn't even started yet.

I looked up, almost hitting the back of my head on the table, and saw the man's name tag: Eddie Kay! *The* Eddie Kay, the legendary organizer from the radical New York City health care workers union

District 1199. I had never met Eddie Kay before, but I had been taught to organize at 1199 Pennsylvania, partly through stories told *about* Eddie by organizers he had trained. And virtually all of these stories involved Eddie yelling at people for doing things wrong.

This was my chance to get yelled at myself—BY EDDIE KAY!

"Eddie Kay! I want you to tell me how I'm screwing up this meeting, but first I want to tell you that I learned to organize by hearing stories about your organizing at 1199P!" I gave him my organizers' genealogy, knowing that this was all going to lead to him really coming down hard on me. He now knew he was dealing with someone who had been indoctrinated into the old lefty New York organizers culture. If an elder is not yelling at you, it means he or she did not take you seriously.

"No, no, no, no, no, no, no, no, no! You can't be an 1199 organizer. You have completely blown this meeting before it even started."

"Because I did not sign everyone in when they walked through the door," I said.

"OK, so now I have even lost more respect for you because you are telling me that you knew the mistake that you were making when you were making it. Explain yourself! If this is the best Bernie has, then I'll tell you what: We are doomed," Eddie said.

I didn't explain. I just asked Eddie to watch the meeting until the end and see if he still thought we had made a mistake then.

It was one of the best barnstorms ever (except that, as usual, I got a little carried away and went on for way too long in my part of the agenda). But we had some other amazing speakers: Cesar Vargas from our Latino outreach team and Brookelynne Moseley, a young African American veteran whom I met when she hosted a small barnstorm at the VFW post that she commanded in Lawrence, Kansas. Brookelynne was there to get trained on the barnstorm mass-meeting model because she had just been hired to become the campaign's Kansas state coordinator.

Then I called Eddie Kay up to speak, despite my fear that he might go on for ninety minutes and there would be nothing I could do about it. But he gave a short speech that gave everyone chills and ended by insulting me several times in front the whole crowd. Don't worry, all in love! I was honored and flattered to be abused by Eddie right in the heart of Brooklyn.

We finally got to the work of the barnstorm and a huge number of people stepped up to lead phone banks. Each one pitched their event with its special twist: a mix of hipsters promising good microbrew beer, immigrant families promising homemade food, and Brooklynites of Bernie's generation promising a genuine Bernie accent.

And then we got everyone else on their feet signing up for the events. And about 90 percent of them did! I knew Eddie would be proud.

"Eddie," I said at the end, "We got nearly everyone signed up, not just on attendance sheets, but for actual shifts to do work!"

"Whatever!" Eddie said, "You should have taken attendance."

He might have been wondering how all those signups on host sheets would make it into our database. But we would soon scan all the sheets with our mobile phones and send them to our volunteer data entry team, who would start entering the data that night.

The Brooklyn beer garden barnstorm was a small but perfect example of how an old best practice can become irrelevant in the face of a new way of doing things. It's not that we had any problem with doing attendance signups, but at that venue with such a big crowd, hundreds of people would have been standing in line in the freezing cold. And the meeting would have started late because the line to get in was so long! We knew we could get rid of the attendance sheets because we generally had 90 percent of attendees signing up for events. What was more valuable than knowing who was there was knowing who was ready to get to work.

Your organizing will continually change for the better if you're always willing to throw out old practices and replace them with new, better ways of doing things. If our staff and volunteers had stuck with all the best practices that they had grown up with as organizers, or even just gotten used to in their first months of the campaign, we never would have been able to even contemplate barnstorms and many other parts of our program.

We also dropped formal trainings from our program, something that's always been a staple of serious voter contact programs. When we began barnstorming in Tennessee, our first ask was for volunteers to bring a huge number of people together for a weekend training. We also scheduled two trainings in Massachusetts following a stadium rally, hoping to capture enthusiasm coming out of that event. But it was nearly impossible to get people to show up for either training. And while everyone who did show up enjoyed the trainings, we needed thousands of people to be doing effective voter contact across the country. It was easy to see that traditional trainings were not going to be an effective way of getting to those numbers.

So we threw out formal trainings and built a whole lot of informal training resources into our program. Our biggest breakthrough was when Ceci Hall started knocking herself out doing three or four webinar trainings with potential phone bankers each day (still working as a volunteer while we worked to get her hire approved). Soon, Ceci had trained several thousand phone bankers on these webinars. Then we recorded one of the webinars and posted it online and that helped thousands more.

People learn differently now than they did a decade ago. They are used to figuring things out themselves through a little online research or by watching amateur videos on YouTube. In the Bernie campaign, we learned that people who are really ready to get to work can self-train online and then simply ask questions in Slack or on a live chat or get support from volunteer peers. From our experience, we knew that a lot of people who come to in-person trainings never actually get to work; our new approach was far more efficient.

There was one "best practice" that became a huge source of friction between the distributed organizers and the field department. An orthodoxy has developed in Democratic Party electoral field organizing over the past several election cycles that "if it's not in the VAN, it didn't happen." It comes from the legitimate reason that campaigns need to ensure the work that field organizers and volunteers say they are doing actually takes place and that the results of things like door knocking make their way into the campaign's voter file or central database. It also prevents wasting time revisiting voters and allows analysts to make sure the campaign is communicating with the highest-priority voters to calibrate predictive models for targeting.

That orthodoxy, however, created problems for scaling our distributed organizing team because so much of our work was being done by volunteers who did not have access to the VAN. We definitely needed all of our contacts with voters to be logged in the VAN. But there was no way to get those data—which volunteers were making which calls and when they were making them—into the VAN because our volunteers did not have access to the VAN. Therefore, we did record all those data, and made them available to our data team, but since they were not necessary for GOTV, we didn't slow down our growth just so we could get those unnecessary data into the VAN.

Normally, all volunteering would be run out of a brick-and-mortar office run by staff, so volunteering data would get into the database (usually in late-night, sleep-depriving data entry sessions). It was still true that the work our volunteers were doing needed to be tracked in perfect detail. But because they didn't have access to the VAN and because our tiny national data team in Burlington didn't have the bandwidth to process and import all those data, we had to accomplish the purpose of the best practice through updated means.

Perhaps the most profound example of the need to overthrow best practices has to do with targeting. Modern campaigns have become obsessed with using big data to microtarget narrow slices of the electorate so that scarce voter contact resources can be aimed most effectively at the right group of voters. But in a few state contests, we found that our voter contact resources were not scarce, at least not when it came to phone banking. We had a national calling machine that could be focused on an individual race (for example, Nevada or Michigan). We found that we had enough people dialing that we could call every voter—*every voter!*—every day. We wouldn't reach all of them, of course, but since we couldn't repeatedly call our target voters ten times per night, it made sense to simply call everyone each night.

It could be difficult to broach the subject of calling everyone with the data and field teams for whom so much of their careers had been devoted to learning to aim at a small target. If we had started earlier and figured out barnstorming earlier, we would have had a much larger capacity and may have even been able to dispense with targeting when it came to phone banking for the whole election.

What makes throwing out old best practices difficult is that you get yelled at, like I did with Eddie Kay. You'll get yelled at by your bosses, your colleagues, your volunteers, and even sometimes the press. If you lose, people will identify your rejection of orthodoxy as one of the reasons you lost, even in cases where it was something that got you closer to victory. So you have to decide whether you care more about acceptance from the "best practice" experts or the success of your revolution. We hope you choose the revolution!

The Revolution Is Not Just Bottom Up; It's Peer to Peer

★ becky ★

The best movements invite great leaders from the base into a structure where all leaders work together as peers to reach their full potential and win. Your base contains many talented and experienced people; treating them as peers is the best way to attract them into leadership; working with them as you would with paid colleagues is the best way to keep them in leadership while bringing out the best in them.

"Change never takes place from the top down, it comes from the bottom up" was a major applause line in Bernie's stump speech. Whenever he would say it, people would cheer. We knew that "bottom up" meant all of us.

"Bottom up" described our battle of ideas with the establishment, but it didn't describe how a huge part of the organizing on the campaign actually worked. "Peer to peer" more accurately describes the concept at the heart of our distributed organizing program.

Zack and I have led careers at the intersection of technology and organizing. We're tuned in to and have been influenced by how technology is changing the way people live their lives. This is important if you're an organizer because you have to meet most people where they "live."

When the telephone was invented and organizers started using the telephone to talk to people, they didn't call them telephone organizers. But as communication technologies have evolved, there's been a tendency to put people who adapt to technology in a special department and associate them with the medium rather than how they use that medium as a vehicle for good old-fashioned organizing.

We know from behavioral political science experiments that contacts with voters are powerful to the extent that they are personal. This means a person-to-person conversation has the highest impact and an impersonal broadcast ad or broadcast robocall ranks among the least-effective tactics for mobilizing voters.

The importance of the personal contact is also true when it comes to organizing volunteers. We had a 40 percent response rate when we sent peer-to-peer text messages to Bernie supporters asking them to volunteer. This doesn't mean that 40 percent of the people volunteered, it means that 40 percent of the people we texted engaged with us in a conversation about volunteering. It was an exponentially higher rate than we saw when we sent an email and many times higher the rate we achieved when we made phone calls to prospective volunteers.

So on the Bernie distributed organizing team, peer-to-peer communication was both at the heart of our voter contact and central to how we managed the volunteer organization behind the voter contact numbers.

Peer to peer is a geeky term that has its roots in distributed file-sharing computing networks. In the context of the Bernie campaign it's a pretty good description of how volunteers and staff worked in a network rather than in a pyramidal hierarchy. There was not much of a center to our organizing—the organizing was distributed—but there was definitely a central plan.

There was another way that the concept of peer to peer profoundly shaped the work of our team: staff on the distributed organizing team saw our volunteer leaders as peers.

I'll give you just one example from our staff—an organizer we called Texas Zack. He had to be called Texas Zack because the distributed team already had a Zack—Zack Exley. Zack Malitz grew up in Austin, Texas, but went to college at CUNY in New York City and became deeply involved in his adopted state's antifracking movement. I met Zack back in 2012, when CREDO was searching for a new environmental organizer. He was twenty-four years old back then but had a pragmatic idealism rarely seen in activists his age. We hired him to lead CREDO's members in the fight against hydraulic fracturing, and he soon established himself as one of the nation's foremost antifracking activists.

Soon after I left CREDO for the Bernie campaign, Texas Zack talked his way onto his home state's Bernie operation. At the Bernie headquarters in Austin, he put in fourteen-hour days on the campaign, punctuated by coffee, which eventually faded into Lone Star tall boys at a café/bar near the office called Rio Rita. Still he found the time to set up his own state-based organizing laboratory, which would lead to one of the highest-impact discoveries of the campaign.

The request came in from Texas Zack in the middle of January. Was there anyone on the national team who could help him with a potentially game-changing experiment? He realized he and others on the small Texas staff simply didn't have the time and resources to barnstorm the far corners of Texas to recruit volunteer teams for GOTV. But he suspected that volunteers would travel at their own expense to organize the meetings that staff simply couldn't get to.

He had invited a group of Texas super volunteers who had already proven that they were ready to work to attend a special meeting at the Austin Bernie headquarters on January 21. Texas Zack had only been to a few barnstorms himself. Could any barnstorm expert on the national distributed organizing team possibly attend and help him run this training?

There were two things I loved about this request. First, the best experiments to run are those that probably won't work, but if they do work, they represent not just a small incremental improvement but a breakthrough for growth. This was all that, plus it would be quick to test and analyze the results so we could start building a national program around it if it was successful. Second, the day he made the request, the high in Burlington was 19° F, while the high in Austin was fifty degrees higher—and as it turned out, I was the only one who was available to be there on the day the training had been planned.

So I made plans to fly down to Texas from Burlington before I had to be in Iowa for a major volunteer event. January 21 was a weirdly momentous date. It was both the anniversary of the disastrous Citizens United Supreme Court decision and my birthday.

I headed down to Austin with low expectations. It wasn't that I didn't think volunteers could lead barnstorms. It was more that I was concerned that volunteers leading barnstorms would recruit fewer volunteer shifts because making a "hard ask" to a room full of strangers is one of the hardest tasks for an organizer. If the ask by the volunteer host was only half as effective as that of staff, it simply wouldn't be worth the work to recruit and train the hosts and then do turnout for the meetings. That said, if Texas Zack was right and this was successful, then the possibilities for scale were enormous. It was high risk, high reward, and well worth the side trip to Austin.

Texas Zack picked me up at the airport and it was nice to meet up with him again—we hadn't seen each other since my departure from CREDO several months prior. I crashed, and we planned to meet up the next morning at El Chilito, a taco stand near his office.

There we ate migas tacos and drank coffee at an outside picnic table while Texas Zack explained his vision. There were sixteen volunteers coming. All of them had successfully hosted phone banks and nearly all of them had already attended a barnstorm led by staff in Austin. There were locations like Abilene, Waco, and Nacogdoches where there were pockets of volunteers waiting to be activated by the campaign. But we just weren't reaching them effectively with email. And as a staffer with crazy responsibilities already, he simply didn't have time to drive three hundred miles across the state to hold a meeting. The organizer in Houston already had so much turf that she could barely cover the vast Houston exurbs let alone make it out to east Texas. But in Austin, he had volunteers who were willing to travel at their own expense. Because we had designed the barnstorm to be replicable by local staff, there was sufficient documentation, plus a literal script the volunteer could rely on. "I think this could really work," said Texas Zack. "And if it does work and we roll it out nationally, this could go really big."

Texas Zack looks every bit the twenty-seven-year-old hipster he is. Skinny jeans, big black thick-framed glasses, and a mop of unruly hair on the top of his head but the sides cut fashionably short. He is also a climate activist. You'd think a guy like this would be all about exclusive lingo, with very strong opinions about what's in and what's out. You'd think he'd be the kind of person who might eschew any coffee that's not single-origin slow-drip prepared. But one of the things that makes him such a great organizer is that he doesn't see himself as the expert and everyone else as those who benefit from his expertise. He sees expertise as something that everyone willing to work hard brings in some form or other to the revolution.

Texas Zack saw the volunteer leaders who were coming to the meeting at the Austin headquarters that evening as his peers in the movement we were all building together. This isn't always the way it goes with hipster, college-educated, elite organizers. Let's face it, this isn't *usually* the way it goes. Most of the people coming had life experiences that would allow them to perform duties on the campaign and connect with others in *more* powerful ways than any of the paid staffers. It wasn't Texas Zack's job to be the manager of the volunteers, or to put them on a pedestal in a vague and abstract way as the people who made this all possible. His job was to empower them as fellow leaders in the movement, which meant trusting them to do valuable work, providing them with strategy and resources, and then asking them to do a lot in return and holding them accountable to do it.

This is a crucial principle. We were all building this movement together, and for the movement to truly work and grow as big as we needed it to be, staff and the volunteer leaders, who it's important to note vastly outnumbered staff, would necessarily be peers in a network, not task rabbits to be managed.

That evening at the Victorian cottage that served as campaign headquarters for the Bernie campaign in Texas, sixteen volunteers slowly filed in to take seats in a circle. As we went around the circle briefly introducing ourselves, I realized that one of the volunteers was well known to the national distributed organizing staff. Barbara

Fetonte, a petite silver-haired senior and longtime labor activist, got up to hug a tall, husky, sandy-haired young man as he arrived. He looked nearly two feet taller than her. As it turned out they had met volunteering for the campaign. Barbara was somewhat of a campaign legend. As soon as Bernie announced his candidacy, before anyone was even thinking about the campaign in Texas, she and her husband Danny launched a drive to collect all the signatures necessary to put Bernie's name on the ballot in the primary. Over the course of the campaign she would hold over fifty events in her home. At one of these events, she'd met the man she hugged. He was a US Army combat medic and Afghanistan war veteran who had never been involved in a political campaign before but read about Bernie online and decided it was time to do something. Andrew Hansen went to map.berniesanders.com and put in his zip code. There was an event happening at Barbara's house, so he dutifully knocked on the door at the appointed time and, after that first experience volunteering, threw himself into the campaign. I didn't know it then, but he would soon drive nine hours across the state to host a barnstorm in Alpine, Texas, and eventually ended up at the Democratic National Convention as a member of the Texas delegation for Bernie.

To a one, these were all ridiculously committed and talented people. This was by design. Texas Zack had handpicked people who had already proven themselves by doing the work. There wasn't a single person in the group whose favorite way to participate in activism was by listening to themselves talk. Together we went through the detailed guide on how to run a barnstorm, including the script. We explained how each part of the agenda had been developed, why it was important, and how following the format of the meeting exactly was key to its success. We explained the best ways to find a venue (start with community rooms at libraries, try local union halls, and so on). Everyone was worried about "the ask." What if no one stood up when they asked who could be a hero and become the person who hosts the recurring local voter contact events we needed them to establish? Texas Zack explained that we always worried about that part, too, and that the beauty of it was that they weren't asking people to do anything they hadn't already done themselves.

What happened next was astonishing. Though I don't know why it should have been. Texas Zack had a list of a few dozen cities from Abilene to Nacogdoches. He asked everyone to sign up for at least two cities and commit to doing barnstorms in those cities within the next two weeks. They would have to do everything and cover their own expenses. All the campaign would do was to invite people from the email list to attend. And he said that they could stay connected to each other and to Texas Zack to help each other through the process. They all went over to the signup sheet and started divvying up the cities until nearly every city on the list was taken.

It was the best birthday present I could have imagined.

Out of the sixteen people who attended the meeting that night fifteen led barnstorms. That's a response rate of 94 percent. What's more, when Texas Zack compared subsequent volunteer shifts completed as a result of those volunteer-led barnstorms with barnstorms led by paid staffers on the Texas team, outcomes were virtually identical. His hunch had been right. There was very little difference between the paid staff and the super volunteers when it came down to organizing the people into voter contact. We were truly building this movement together.

Texas Zack would soon be promoted to the national team, where he rolled out the volunteer barnstorm hosting model countrywide. He started by inviting phone bank hosts to livestream trainings, and soon we had hundreds of these meetings happening all over the country. Eventually, with a huge lift from Alexandra Rojas, one of the interns from Orange Coast College, who was promoted to digital field manager, and Mary Nishimuta, a volunteer management consultant from Frankfort, Kentucky, the campaign held one thousand barnstorm meetings. Incredibly, 650 of them were led by volunteers. None of this would have happened if Texas Zack didn't engage in every task with the assumption that the volunteers he was working with were his peers, coleaders in this movement that we were building together.

The barnstorm was a perfect storm of the peer-to-peer style of networked organizing. It became a center of our distributed organizing strategy on the Bernie campaign because it accomplished three things. First, it was how we scaled our ability to connect individual volunteers with individual voters by creating phone banks, and in some case setting up canvasses or recruiting people for our peer-to-peer texting program. Second, it was about connecting volunteers to each other so they could work in teams, share advice, and practice solidarity. Finally, as we empowered volunteers to grow the program by running and not just attending the barnstorms, it was how we demonstrated the relationship of staff to key volunteer leaders as peers.

Repeat "Rinse and Repeat"

★ zack ★

Mass movements can move mountains if you give each person a shovel. If you give your base some effective tactics that they can "rinse and repeat" to make progress on a strategic plan, then your movement will be very effective. But to make a revolution, you also need to discover a rinse-and-repeatable way to grow.

For something to grow, a lot of different kinds of processes have to be present. An important one is repetition. One way that organizers refer to the work of creating the cycles of repetition necessary to grow organizations is "rinse and repeat."

In my first organizing job, the union president gave us a very simple task—visit workers at home to collect union cards—and we knew our job was to repeat it as many times as possible each day. Any strategizing or decision making about the campaign was done by our union president, who was leading the campaign, not by us. Therefore, we never got stuck. As the campaign went on, a few other tasks were added to the cycle, but the job of us organizers was always simple and repeatable.

Since then, in every job where I've managed teams, I always wanted my staff and volunteers to experience that same productive bliss I had in my first job. I usually tried to recreate it by holding teams accountable to numbers. Occasionally this worked, but most often it left teams frustrated when their numbers didn't take off. For some reason I couldn't accept that I needed to give them something that was easy to repeat. Sometimes it felt as though the problem was that there never seemed to be any task to give them that they could repeat and that was as clear and simple as collecting union cards.

For example, at Wikipedia I had a team that was supposed to get our volunteer editor community growing again after a period of stagnation and then decline. All kinds of programs were created to foster and mentor editors, and we held staff accountable to numbers to measure success of those programs. But they did not take off. In hindsight, I see that regardless of the difficulty in doing so, I should have found some easily repeatable tasks to put people on to start with.

This is one of many reasons why it was so critical that Becky joined our campaign. I remember when she said on one of her first days, "We just need to figure out how to get the 'rinse and repeat' cycle going with the volunteers," the lesson I should have learned a long time ago finally snapped into place in my mind.

At that time, Corbin and I had been asking volunteers to hold outreach events every week. For the record, we would have rather asked them to phone bank, but we still didn't have the dialer or any list of voters that the field program wanted us to call. In lieu of that, we thought we could help volunteer groups grow and multiply by encouraging them to do what so many were already doing: signing up volunteers and registering voters at fairs, markets, and other public places.

We were holding volunteers accountable to numbers. We invited all state organizers onto massive conference calls every week where we reported last week's numbers, and asked people to go out there and do more. Unfortunately, the movement didn't grow very much each week that way.

Becky knew why: There was nothing simple that volunteers could do over and over that would lead to more events. There was no "rinse and repeat" activity in our program. The phrase "rinse and repeat" refers to the instructions on many shampoo bottles: "Lather, Rinse, and Repeat." In marketing lore, there was a point at which someone added the word "repeat" to the instructions, leading to massively increased sales.

The phrase is apt because what you're looking for as a leader in organizing is something that your staff and volunteers can easily do over and over, as many times as they have the energy for. Something like logging in to a virtual call center and doing call after call. Something not like organizing a benefit concert, which can only happen every once in a while and requires extensive coordination with others.

Once we had the dialer up and running—and even before that, with manual dialing—our number of engaged volunteers who were actually accomplishing something started going up in a linear growth pattern. People were calling from home, from house parties, even while stuck in traffic.

Here's what makes getting to rinse and repeat so hard: It takes non-rinse and repeat work to set up a rinse and repeat process. To get phone banking up and running at scale, we had to figure out how to effectively recruit hosts, then get RSVPs for the events that went up on the map, and all the while hash out implementation of hundreds of other details like optimizing the dialer software, writing guides, making training videos, and so much more. But once all that was done, volunteers were soon on their way to making millions of calls, the rinse and repeat cycle.

Rinse and repeat has always been at the center of organizing, and it is a central staple of small organizing. In my career as an organizer, as I tried to figure out how to get back to mass movement organizing, I knew we had to do something more than simple rinse and repeat processes. I knew that huge numbers of volunteers everywhere, from all backgrounds, were going to need to take on—and were already capable of taking on—big strategic leadership roles on their own.

But I was putting the cart before the horse when I failed to start by rolling out a rinse and repeat activity that would build our movement—something that everyone could do wherever they were. Becky's insistence that we start with simple phone banking—because there is no growth without rinse and repeat—changed everything for us.

Thanks to one layer of rinse and repeat, we had a linear growth pattern. The problem was that, if we extrapolated that linear growth pattern through the primaries, it didn't add up to enough activity to make the difference we needed to put Bernie over the top in key contests.

We needed to add another growth process. But growth processes rely on rinse and repeat. So we needed another layer of rinse and repeat on top of the one we already had. We needed to find something that would radically increase the volume of phone banking, and then do that over and over. That, of course, was the barnstorm.

Again, it was Becky who led the way in making this happen. Corbin and I had been out there doing barnstorms on our own and telling the rest of the team about them, but Becky led the effort to package the barnstorm into something that all of our staff could spearhead on their own across the country. It helped to get us all together to watch barnstorms in person, first in Seattle, then in New York where we did nine events in one weekend. We began doing a second fifteen-minute "stand up" meeting at the end of our team call each morning for anyone involved in barnstorms, where we'd talk about new tactics that were working.

Here again, it took a lot of non–rinse and repeat work to turn the barnstorm into a rinse and repeat activity for our staff. We had to set up all sorts of volunteer teams and new tech tools to support staff in getting around the country, booking venues, and so on. Meanwhile, we also had to keep up with and support the explosion of organizing events that was coming out of the barnstorms.

Only after we got a linear growth path going with a simple rinse and repeat process—one that practically anyone could participate in—was it possible to set up a higher-level rinse and repeat cycle with barnstorms that would repeatedly bump up the growth curve.

But with a limited number of staff who could do barnstorms, we had not actually switched into permanent exponential growth—the kind of growth we needed to build a voter contact machine that could actually talk to every voter in all the Super Tuesday states to knock down our opponent's big-money "firewall."

A goal that big sounds impossible and would have been laughed off by any experienced field person. We told volunteers at barnstorms that we wanted to get there. The volunteers believed it was possible because they saw how many people had shown up ready to work. They were just waiting to see whether we could organize the conditions that would fully utilize them. And part of what motivated the crowds to sign up was that we were asking them to join a voter contact machine actually big enough to win on Super Tuesday, and March 15, and in New York and California—in other words, on all the primary days where television was supposed to be the only effective strategy because it was thought to be impossible to build a voter contact organization big enough to make a difference. We were asking volunteers to do something big, and they were ready to go for it.

We realized eventually that we probably could have held a barnstorm every week in any city, transforming what we had treated before as a one-time event into a routine, rinse and repeat volunteer-intake session.

But who could hold these? The first volunteer-led barnstorm was a renegade event held by Nina Sherwood in Stamford, Connecticut. After she attended our Brooklyn event (the one with Eddie Kay that we described in "Rule 16: Best Practices Become Worst Practices") she said, "This is amazing. We want to do these all over Connecticut."

Corbin and I talked with her a couple of times on the phone and sent her some materials that our team had been using internally. She held her own barnstorm, and she sent us a video of it at our request. Lo and behold: It went great, and they created a bunch of new phone banks out of the event.

But it was essentially a one-off event. I missed the obvious next move: Turn it into a rinse and repeat activity that an unlimited number of volunteers could do.

Luckily, in a completely unconnected moment of organizing brilliance, Zack Malitz came up with the same idea for volunteer-led barnstorms and recruited Becky from the national team to help him pull off an experiment that, if successful, could be replicated. After testing his way into success at the state level, Texas Zack (as we called him on the campaign) turned volunteer-led barnstorming into a fully rinse and repeat activity.

Unfortunately, the clock on our campaign began to run out when this program was just beginning to pick up steam. And this is one reason why we felt it was so important to write this book. We showed that thousands of volunteers could be put to work doing effective voter contact work. But we were on the verge of showing that hundreds of thousands could be engaged this way.

Rinse and repeat has a role in any campaign. Think about how Bill McKibben and 350.org took a one-day photo-op civil disobedience protest (getting arrested in front of the White House to send a message to the president) and turned it into two weeks of daily arrests of a seemingly endless supply of folks willing to do something big to stop the Keystone XL pipeline. The more people got arrested, the more people wanted to get arrested. The arrests stopped after two weeks, but they could have continued in rinse and repeat mode for a year had there been the money to support the dedicated and exhausted staff. A rinse and repeat activity could also be something as simple as transforming a so-called "day of action" to generate calls to your local legislators into a month of calls spaced out throughout the day every day. When a tactic works, stick with it. Your people get better at it, you refine your processes, and you have the potential for growth.

We hope you take this chapter seriously if you're the manager of the next insurgent revolutionary presidential campaign, but even more so if you're running a local issue campaign, community organization, environmental crusade, or union. Look for rinse and repeat activities that will grow your campaign. Then look for additional rinse and repeat processes that will expand the number of people doing the work. Good luck!

There's No Such Thing as a Single-Issue Revolution

★ becky ★

The revolution is about everything. The people live in communities affected by all the issues, and all of our struggles are connected. That's why there can be no single-issue revolution. What's more, it's going to take all of us, each motivated by the issues that directly affect us, working together to build the revolution.

Bernie Sanders wasn't the movement. He was in the movement. This movement is something we are building together. This is truly our revolution.

All of our struggles are connected. There can be no single-issue revolution.

You can't build a mass movement around a single policy goal. Amazingly, this is almost universally understood by people under twenty-five years of age. Meanwhile, people who work in Washington, DC, or in the nonprofit industrial complex tend to use the word "intersectional" a lot, but when it comes to putting time and resources behind other people's struggles, they don't follow through for the most part. Even if they buy into the concept in practice, they tend to suffer from the tyranny of DC's absurdly low expectations for what is possible.

The Bernie Sanders Latino outreach team was home to some fiercely talented organizers. One of them, Cesar Vargas, brought this rule home to me when I was at an event with him in Phoenix, Arizona. Cesar was a well-known DREAMer and cofounder of DREAM Action Coalition who joined the campaign in its early days. He helped lead the push that forced President Obama's executive actions on immigration, including deferred deportation for undocumented people like himself who were brought to the United States as children and were at risk of deportation to a country they had never known. Cesar was exceptional, so it shouldn't have surprised me that despite becoming the first undocumented lawyer to be approved to practice law in New York State, he was working 24/7 traveling the country to bring Bernie's message to Latino communities in key states.

Cesar's title at the Bernie campaign included the word "strategist," but it's important to note that first and foremost he was an organizer of extraordinary talents. He spent much of his time organizing Latino town halls in city after city, bringing people together to hear him explain Bernie's message, and then organizing them into door-to-door canvasses. Always dapper, despite the frenetic life of a campaigner that means long days punctuated by short nights in cheap motels or supporter housing, I remember him as always being turned out in a sharp blue blazer over a Bernie 2016 T-shirt, jeans, and loafers. Despite his law degree, Cesar proudly filled his Facebook feed with videos of himself heading out on turf to door knock in Latino communities all along the campaign trail. This was a man who cared about getting things done.

Cesar explained to me that too often campaigns going after the Latino vote thought the only thing they had to talk to Latino audiences about was immigration policy. But in reality, a lot of the families he talked with on the campaign trail cared most about universal health care and free public college. They were also concerned about climate change. Yes, they cared deeply about immigration reform, but Latino families shouldn't be treated as single-issue voters. They were facing the same challenges as the majority of Americans, and of course, all of our struggles are connected.

I heard the same thing from students. Hannah Fertig was a cofounder of Buffs for Bernie, a student group at the University of

Colorado Boulder. I met her at a giant barnstorm rally in Denver. She gave me a button with the group's logo—an illustration of Bernie Sanders riding a unicorn with rainbow lasers shooting out of his fingertips. Incredibly, Hannah had come to the Denver barnstorm because she wanted to be extra prepared for the barnstorm we would be doing the very next night in Boulder that she was not only excited to attend but was helping to plan.

Hannah was eventually hired onto the campaign first as an intern and then promoted as a staffer. According to Hannah, it was insulting for Clinton surrogates to be suggesting that young people were for Bernie because they wanted free stuff—referring derogatorily to Bernie's call for free public college, a position that Clinton eventually moved toward. "Students support free college tuition, but it's not even in their top three reasons for supporting Bernie," she explained. "When we ask students why they want Bernie to be president, they talk about climate change, followed by money in politics, then racial justice. Making public colleges and universities tuition-free is probably fourth on the list."

For most of the Bernie supporters I met on the campaign trail, there was no one issue that captured their support. It was that they shared Bernie's political analysis. Bernie ran on an idea: Power is concentrated in the hands of a tiny elite, and ordinary people have to struggle to take back their government. That struggle is what he called the political revolution. He proposed changes the country desperately needs, and he was honest that he would need a movement of millions of people to be with him to make that change possible.

All of our struggles are connected. There's no universal health care without immigration reform. The undocumented will operate in the shadows. If health care is a human right, we also have to deal with our broken immigration system so everyone has access to the medical care they need. In the United States, income inequality is a direct legacy of slavery. Until we deal with structural racism, we won't be able to address rising income inequality. Climate change is contributing to war when drought contributes to civil unrest. Curtailing of our civil liberties through government surveillance gives police departments tools to suppress the movement to defend black lives and the work of antifracking activists. We won't be able to move closer to full employment in the United States without a commitment to moving to 100 percent renewable energy in a short period of time.

The elites are doing better than ever. But the vast majority of people in the United States are losing ground and they are hurting. The reasons are interconnected. The solutions are interconnected, too. The movement that wins the solutions will necessarily be big and it will have to include everybody.

Let's say you don't buy the kumbaya about the issues being interconnected, and you only care about one issue—climate, for example, or money in politics. As an organizer, you have to recognize that no one lives a single-issue life. We're human, and we're affected by everything. To make the changes we need to see on climate or on getting money out of politics, we'll need to fight for those changes alongside the vast majority of the people. For that to happen, the revolution still has to be about immigration and structural racism and abortion rights because the revolution has to be huge, and we won't be able to recruit all the people we need to join us if we don't talk about all the issues at once.

Think about it. Presidential campaigns get big not just because it's a national election but because they are about most (though not all) of the issues. This approach needs to be adopted across the board in our social movements, issue advocacy campaigns, and in the nonprofit sector in general. Most community organizers have been trained to try to identify and tap into a narrowly defined self-interest. In big organizing we expand that to what is broadly in the interest of everyone. That doesn't mean finding a lowest common denominator across everyone you are trying to reach. It means taking on all the issues all at once.

This also doesn't mean we can't work on single-issue campaigns. People who care deeply about one issue in particular can still act in solidarity with other movements, and we can all work together in moments when action is urgent or progress suddenly becomes possible. We're all part of a revolution, and revolution is by its nature big enough to include everyone's struggle.

RULE 20

Get Ready for the Counterrevolution (to Include Your Friends)

★ becky ★

First they ignore you, then they laugh at you, then they start posting mean comments on your Facebook timeline. When you're fighting for radical change, and you get close to winning, all kinds of people—including many you thought were allies—will begin attacking you. You will be surprised, confused, and lose precious time and focus if you're not prepared for the counterrevolution.

In the barnstorm mass meetings we conducted across the country, I would ask the crowd, "Does anyone here have friends or family who tell you they are with Bernie on all the issues, but they're not supporting him because they don't think he can win?"

It was always an intensely emotional moment for the crowd. Everyone's hands went up. The shared frustration was palpable. To complete the catharsis, I would reply, "They say that to me, too! I tell them that I didn't quit my job and go on the campaign because I didn't think Bernie could win! If enough of us get involved, we can win this thing!" Then everyone would laugh, and we would all confirm to each other that Bernie could really win this!

The truth is, it was worse than that. Whenever you try to do something big—or try to do things differently—there are going to be conflicts, politics, and drama. Especially if you call it revolution! It starts with derision or dismissal at first, when you're easy to ignore. But if you start to show success, and it looks like you really might be about to change things, that's when they come down on you like a ton of bricks and the counterrevolution begins in earnest.

The counterrevolution is a real thing. It's the movement to squash revolutionary trends that rises up in unexpected ways whenever we're on the cusp of real change. And it probably will include your friends, even those you wouldn't expect.

Most of us knew people who purported to share the values Bernie campaigned on. And we were depressed to learn how many of them chose a status quo candidate who promised only incremental improvements on some issues (and serious backsliding on others, such as Wall Street accountability and wars of choice in the Middle East) over the candidate who had campaigned on a platform of radical change.

What made the counterrevolution worse was the behavior of a subset of those who said they were with us on the issues but were supporting Clinton in the primary. At first, they simply dismissed Bernie by saying he couldn't win and often invoked the fact that it would be historic for a woman to win a major party nomination. Then when Bernie started surging in the polls, it became more insulting. People who supported Bernie, even women, were painted as sexist "bros" simply for disagreeing with Clinton on the issues. That certainly happened to me.

This was truly counterrevolutionary and infernal: painting the supporters of a feminist, democratic, socialist, political revolution as sexist defenders of the patriarchy! It was as if there was some kind of unconscious externalization process running and they were projecting the dissonance between their own purported progressive values and their public endorsement of Clinton onto the people who were lining up behind Bernie, the candidate whose politics were closest to their own!

The upside to the counterrevolution is that it is a pretty effective filter for identifying who truly wants to work for change. The counterrevolution pops up whenever you're fighting for big change against entrenched interests. When someone who you think would be on your side tries to get you to soften your message or ask for something smaller, that might be the counterrevolution. It often manifests itself when someone who you think is your ally (perhaps a politician) says that it is not a good time to be pressing for change. "If you ask for the big thing, I might not be able to win the small thing," the politician (or someone on their staff) says.

Sometimes people who have revolutionary values join the counterrevolution—this can be for several reasons: They have a career that could be hurt by joining the revolution, their friends are counterrevolutionaries, or they have a psychological investment in nuance that prevents them from seeing the big picture and traps them in a reflexive incrementalism. Those of us who were working for the political revolution may also have inspired a backlash from some people who were truly progressive but supported Clinton. In some ways, they seemed to be suppressing their fear of missing out (FOMO) and then projecting it on to us (for example, calling us "Bernie Bros"). As Bernie became an undeniable cultural force for revolution, progressives supporting Clinton were feeling left out. They were on the winning team—at no point was Bernie the front-runner—but they were acting like sore losers. Perhaps the cognitive dissonance simply got the best of them.

Counterrevolutionaries are almost always devotees of small organizing, while revolutionaries practice big organizing. Take note of the counterrevolutionaries when they reveal themselves. They're definitely not allies, and sometimes they even become enemies in a particular political fight. But don't forget to also take note of who is willing to join you not just in speaking up for big change but in fighting for it.

If you're aware of the counterrevolution, it won't take you by surprise. Get ready for it. You can still be friends with people in the counterrevolution. But don't let them distract or dissuade you from the work of making real, big, and lasting change.

Put Consumer Software at the Center

★ becky ★

Consumer software on our computers and mobile devices has transformed how people organize their lives and their interactions with each other, and it is the new expanded terrain on which organizing succeeds or fails. Used well, free and inexpensive tools that are available to everyone can remove friction and enable teams to work across time and distance toward shared goals. A pinch of custom code can bridge whatever critical gaps emerge.

―――――――――

When I came on the Bernie campaign, I was pretty astonished to learn a few things about the email and web platform the campaign was running on. We were using a popular CRM (constituent relationship manager) that's used by lots of campaigns and nonprofits. It was a productized version of the platform that came out of Howard Dean's 2003–2004 run for the presidency, and was then used by Obama in 2008 and 2012. But it was cheap, and that was a highly valued quality on our campaign, especially at the outset when such technology decisions are made.

Organizing took a hit from the platform's inability to run automated A/B tests on subject lines when sending email to more than one hundred thousand people. There was also the event tool—which in all fairness was hardly ever used by most of the software company's clients—which wouldn't allow us to track RSVPs back to the URL a user had clicked on before signing up. Also it would break on a regular basis.

When the Obama campaign used this platform in 2012, they had an army of developers who built custom tools—like "Air Wolf" for creating randomized segments for testing. Our campaign didn't have the developers or resources to do the same.

All these technical limitations of the CRM I found shocking, but I learned to deal with it.

I was the person on our team who knew the most about email production as it turned out. Zack, Claire, Corbin, and others had been coding their own emails before I joined, and quite frankly they were terrible at it. This was causing tension with Revolution Messaging, who handled the day-to-day management of our email list. So I ended up taking this over, and in the early months on the campaign I spent a significant amount of time every day coding and testing all the team's emails. (Thankfully Will Easton took this over when he came on board in January.)

As it turned out, organizers had also been going rogue, creating stealth Google forms to recruit volunteers for smaller-scale tasks instead of building pages in the campaign CRM that were connected to our main database. Even though I recognized how much easier it was to collect and then access information in a Google sheet attached to a Google form, I dutifully told the folks on the distributed team that we would no longer be sending emails out that pointed to Google forms. Everything had to be in the campaign CRM so that we didn't maroon pockets of valuable information all over the Googleverse.

Then came the day, maybe a month after I'd joined the campaign, when I learned that anyone who had a log-in to administer events on the website could download the entire list of anyone who had ever attended an event. This was because the CRM had only a very rudimentary system for setting permissions—it was practically full admin access or nothing when it came to the event tool. At this time

I calculated that there was contact information for more than five hundred thousand of Bernie's best supporters, and I knew there would be soon enough over one million.

As the head of CREDO Action, even I wouldn't have been able to download half a million of our best activists to my desktop without going through a verified process with the vendor to ensure that I wasn't a rogue employee stealing one of my company's most valuable resources—its list of supporters.

But we had given a team of volunteers what we thought was a limited permission access so they could help administer events in the CRM. The reason for this is that a human had to review every event posted to map.berniesanders.com before it went live. Staff simply could not keep up with the thousands of events being posted each week—at some points, one thousand events a day. So we had a dedicated group of volunteers who worked in shifts to vet and approve events as hosts posted them on the web.

How could the enterprise software that large organizations like presidential campaigns use be so terrible? The answer wasn't specific to political campaigns. Anyone who has worked for a large company and been forced to use Microsoft Outlook for their enterprise email rather than the cheaper and far more user-friendly Gmail knows this well. Compared to a lot of the consumer software we're used to using, enterprise software can pretty much suck.

We're at a remarkable moment in the history of technology when cheap consumer technology has far outpaced custom and enterprise tools when it comes to enabling teams to work together. It has to do with the explosion of the need for software that removes friction from team collaboration in an increasingly distributed economy. As it turns out, what works to enable productivity in business can also be used to scale productivity of volunteer engagement.

We realized we couldn't fix our CRM. But we could add a lightweight layer on top of it to ease the biggest sticking points (like not giving volunteers access to downloading the campaign's most valuable supporters!). But what's more, we would simply avoid enterprise or custom software to the extent possible and instead focus on using software platforms, most of them social in nature, that were already serving hundreds of millions of people, that were not slow or buggy, that were designed for extreme ease of use, and that many of our volunteers were already using in their daily lives. Not only were they better tools, but because they were so accessible and widely used, the volunteers we hoped to serve with these tools could help us with the process of configuring them for our organizing purposes.

That meant using mostly free consumer software like Slack, Google Apps, free conference calling, and Trello to organize volunteers around work that took place on platforms that we paid to use but that weren't customized for political campaign work—platforms like our virtual call center software that powered the Bernie Dialer, the peer-to-peer texting app we used in Text for Bernie, and Facebook, which volunteers used for Facebanking, as well, to promote events and help local groups communicate.

We put consumer software, connected by custom coding, at the center of our distributed organizing efforts. And it made all the difference.

The consumer software piece of this rule is something a lot of organizers could put together. For the custom-coding piece, we were lucky enough to get to work with a developer who cared as much about organizing as he did about code. Saikat Chakrabarti was a very early employee on the product team of the giant tech company Stripe, which was founded in 2010 and annually processes billions of dollars of payments online and via mobile apps.

Saikat was inspired by Bernie's message, and he wanted to figure out how he could use his skills as a developer to help Bernie get elected. There happened to be a guy who was known to be pretty connected in Democratic circles on the product-engineering team at Stripe. Zack and I knew Ben Rahn through ActBlue, an organization that's processed more than a billion dollars in small political donations. Ben had dropped out of a doctoral program in theoretical physics to cofound ActBlue with Matt DeBergalis, a computer science graduate of MIT he had met at computer camp in high school. Ben introduced Saikat to Zack, who recruited him to join the Bernie campaign as the director of organizing technology.

Saikat wasn't just a coder on the Bernie campaign. He was a hybrid developer/organizer who brought trenchant thinking about systems to our human as well as our computer assisted processes. He was very soft-spoken, but when he said something, people listened because it was usually something essential that no one had thought of or a unique synthesis of completely logical approaches that, as soon as he said it, the rest of us thought—why didn't I think of that?

Saikat always sought to build the minimally viable product that our volunteers needed rather than the cool tool a software guy might have fun developing. That was the impetus behind his highest-impact project, which he called Ground Control. Ground Control was a snappy user interface that allowed our volunteer teams to do everything and anything we wanted them to do with events without logging in to the campaign CRM. This included, crucially, reviewing, editing, and approving events; creating events and RSVPing attendees from barnstorm sign-in sheets; and mirroring the famous "calendar" from the barnstorm in order to allow creation of multiple events with just a few clicks. It also included an automated way for event hosts to make phone calls and send personal emails to Bernie supporters who lived near their events. It was game changing. This may sound overly dramatic, but without Saikat's app, we wouldn't have been able to scale our distributed organizing program.

Because we didn't have the people or resources to build everything from scratch, Saikat embraced using off-the-shelf software or, better yet, consumer software first and then employing custom coding to cover any gaps—and he also embraced other volunteer coders who wanted to work to solve the problems we had (not just produce the cool tools they thought we should be using).

Text for Bernie is a great example of how our orientation to consumer software helped us build and maintain a powerful, volunteer-driven voter contact machine.

Text for Bernie's genesis came when Kenneth was introduced to a new peer-to-peer texting app that he thought might be interesting. It's a testament to Kenneth's judgment that he pulled this app out of the tsunami of software pitches that swamp digital teams on presidential campaigns. Kenneth offered to help the Iowa, New Hampshire, and Nevada teams test the app out if they were so inclined. Thankfully,

Iowa digital director Pinky Weitzman was also intrigued. She helped a young field organizer named Zach Fang test it, and immediately they knew they had gotten hold of something powerful. Zach was a fantastic evangelist for the tactic and speeded adoption of the app within the Iowa field team.

When Kenneth saw how many contacts with volunteers the team in Iowa was piling up in a short amount of time, he saw the power of scaling the program for GOTV. Kenneth wanted to go big. With guidance from Kenneth, the national distributed team launched Text for Bernie under tremendous pressure to quickly build the capacity to individually send a million text messages to turn out Bernie voters in the eleven states that voted on Super Tuesday.

It would take over one thousand volunteers working together to pull it off. There was no way we could have made it happen if we were organizing them using the campaign CRM for anything but sending outbound emails to recruit people to join the program. The user flow went through a series of consumer platforms and then the voter contact took place via a texting app. Finally, the campaign flowed the data from the texting app back into our CRM by a series of manual processes that were later automated (and the CRM synched relevant information back to the VAN).

I put Daniel Souweine, a member of the distributed organizing team who had fairly extensive management experience, in charge of meeting the goals Kenneth set. Daniel was a cofounder of the Citizen Engagement Lab, a nonprofit incubator based in the San Francisco Bay Area, and he also founded and served as the director of the organization's climate lab. Daniel is the kind of guy who says little but does a lot. He was scheduled to go on a long-overdue vacation but cancelled his trip when he had the chance to move to Burlington and jump on the Bernie campaign. He had been managing big organizations, so I wondered how he would adapt to the hands-on work that was required of everyone on the team no matter what their previous job title had been (after all, even I got stuck as the person responsible for coding all our team's email for the first few months.) As it turns out, Daniel was a total machine and a great guy to be with in a pressure-cooker campaign environment.

To help Daniel, I assigned him Sam Ghazey, a University of Vermont senior who had been transferred to our team as an intern. Since we didn't have enough staff to give Daniel any kind of assistance, Ghazey (as we called him, since we already had a Sam on the team) was considered draftable—we didn't know if he would be a good organizer. Ghazey was being billed to the intern program, and we saw him as a freebie. He was thrilled to be on Daniel's team, and luckily he turned out to be a hard worker, a technology enthusiast, and a great organizer!

What Daniel and Ghazey built using the principles of organizing that we had developed in launching the Bernie Dialer was nothing short of amazing to me. It was a complex and multilayered volunteer organization that scaled. And it was based almost entirely on consumer software.

I was so impressed by what they had built that I eventually joined the program as a volunteer so I could experience the program from the user's point of view. How and why did this work so insanely well? I'm going to go into detail about the various software platforms so you can see how the sausage was made. But keep in mind that this will be outdated shortly after I write it. The point is not that these programs are great for organizing but that the principle behind using consumer software at the center of our organization helped us build a powerful, connected, and inclusive machine for change.

My point of entry was textforbernie.com. The site was built by Elanor Riley, a volunteer whose enviable day job was working as a web developer at Bell's Brewery in Portage, Michigan. In her spare time she gave lectures on topics like "Fostering Innovation and a Culture of Openness through Crowdsourced Idea Generation." Textforbernie.com was handsomely designed using the Bernie campaign's color scheme and font, but it wasn't hosted on or even associated with berniesanders.com.

Clicking "How to get started" led to a Trello board that was also created and maintained by volunteers. Trello is a visual, intuitive, and easy-to-use online collaboration tool that organizes projects into boards. Boards are made up of cards that can be put in an order and allow people who are signed into the board to make comments.

People use Trello for everything from managing complex software development projects to planning their family vacation.

On the Trello board, cards were organized into four columns—"Start Here," "Rules," "Assignments and Texting," and "Tips and Tricks."

"Start Here" led me through a series of cards that linked to a series of Google docs and YouTube videos, where I was required to self-train by reading a detailed guide and then watching a video webinar.

A subsequent Trello card pushed me to take a quiz that was a simple Google form that tested the knowledge I had gained in the trainings I had just completed. The first question harvested my email address. The last question asked me to agree to abide by the Text for Bernie credo and follow a set of ground rules provided by the campaign. After completing the test successfully (getting 80 percent of the questions right was considered a passing grade), I received an automatic email with the link to join the Text for Bernie Slack and a link to download the app we used for peer-to-peer texting.

Slack is a popular commercial platform that allows for real-time collaboration among teams using either a smartphone app or an app on a computer. Using Slack, just a few paid staffers can direct the work of thousands of volunteers in real time (our Bernie Builders volunteer Slack team had five thousand members at its peak). Volunteers carry the load of countless tasks, simply tagging key super volunteers or staffers when they need direction. Carrying out these conversations in public Slack channels helps educate and direct other volunteers. Slack can be used in a free version at scale or for a minimal cost per month per user.

Slack was not optional for Text for Bernie. Volunteers had to join Slack and learn how to use it if they wanted to participate, because the shift sign-up process depended on Slack usernames with a Slack integration.

I was more than happy to adopt Slack as part of volunteering, as Slack had changed my life when we started using it at CREDO in order to solve the crisis in communication that was caused by too many "damn emails," to use Bernie's turn of phrase. When I logged in to the Text for Bernie Slack—a totally separate Slack team from

Bernie Builders—I was excited to join what I knew was a massive and incredibly vibrant shared staff/volunteer Slack team that eventually boasted over two thousand participants.

Next I was funneled into a newbie Slack channel and that was all I could access. Slack had been so important to managing the program and so many new people were coming in every day that volunteers joining it were first put into kind of a Slack Montessori preschool. I was immediately tagged by a fellow experienced volunteer whose job it was to welcome me into Slack and answer any questions.

Later I found out that the person who had reached out to me on Slack was part of a group of volunteers called text mentors. They had a schedule they managed on their own to ensure the Slack channel was always "staffed." Text mentors asked new volunteers if they had any last questions. Then they asked a couple of questions from the quiz to make sure that you had retained the information from the self-training. Once you passed these hurdles, you would get an invitation to the main assignments channel, where you would be allowed to sign up for a shift.

I was blown away. Not only did I feel welcomed and supported, but I would later see how that onboarding process helped to answer all the beginner questions in a segregated Slack channel so newbies didn't clog up the other threads that were vital to keeping the program running efficiently and at capacity.

Daniel and Ghazey's system was working.

Once I was in the assignments channel, I was able to sign up for shifts in a customized Google sheet. Eventually this Google sheet crumbled under the volume and a custom-built shift schedule that Elanor built for the campaign was used instead. The shift schedule could post notifications back to Slack, letting people know they had an assignment.

Soon I would join the over one thousand Text for Bernie volunteers bobbing amid the waves of Slack, waiting for an assignment like surfers wait for a wave.

Once I had my assignment, I was directed to another Google doc called the "T4B Info doc." This was where information about the day's assignments was posted. It covered frequently asked questions about events, suggesting replies, giving contextual information, and more. Later this was migrated to another Trello board. Because we did this in Google docs and later an additional Trello board, it got more complete as the day went on as volunteers added updated information that others might need based on their interactions as part of their assignment.

Only after I'd consulted that document could I open up the app on my phone and start texting supporters one by one in powerful interactions that started with a script and then went into often awesome free-form conversations with Bernie supporters. I'd be either recruiting for a nearby event or giving them voting information if I had a GOTV assignment. I soon created a script for replying "feel the bern!!!" because many of the interactions were so positive.

It was one the best GOTV volunteer experiences of my career. I credited Daniel and Ghazey with developing the amazing system. But they always deflected credit to their crew of talented, hardworking, and passionate volunteers.

Daniel liked to say that if he was hit by a bus, Text for Bernie could continue to operate without even a momentary stutter because of volunteers like Catherine Aronson. Catherine is a technology executive at Xerox, where she serves as a senior solutions architect working remotely from Panama City, Florida. She is savvy on multiple levels of designing software systems, from UI to data to infrastructure.

Not only was she an incredibly hard worker but she also demonstrated a highly intelligent sense of curiosity. Aside from voting, Catherine had never really been involved in politics when she joined Text for Bernie as an early volunteer. She started out as a texter but soon shifted into a volunteer data manager role (data managers were volunteers who loaded assignments into the Text for Bernie application, and were a volunteer's "go to" resource for assignment-specific issues and questions).

Over time, Catherine became the lead volunteer on the data manager team, and she functioned in essential ways as part of the staff.

In addition to her role as a data manager, Catherine built Text for Bernie's internal data sheet where we crunched numbers from our texting vendor and tracked data exports. She wrote the guide for volunteer platform admins and, according to Daniel, "weighed in on nearly every strategic or tactical decision we made."

We worked with hundreds of volunteers like Catherine on the distributed organizing team. Overwhelmingly new to politics, female, highly intelligent, and working a great job during the day but making time for consistent and meaningful work as part of a hybrid volunteer/staff team. This was only possible because we were working through consumer software platforms that allowed us to coordinate across time and space, and because we were able to leverage occasional custom coding from smart and agile developers like Elanor.

It's worth noting some of the other consumer software platforms that were central to our operation. There's been an emergence of free or low-cost conference calling platforms that have features that are fantastic for organizing and create spaces for volunteers to work together on a regular basis. Not only can you now have hundreds of people organize on no-cost conference calls, but there are low-cost products like Maestro that allow call organizers to segment a mass call into multiple small "rooms"—for example, breaking out by state—that call attendees can self-select by dialing a corresponding number when prompted, and then to join them back into the mass call at a time decided by the organizer.

Forums like Facebook and Reddit allow volunteers to self-organize in communities that paid staff can contribute to but that persist from campaign to campaign. Facebook provides better recruiting and RSVP tools than any commonly used email and web platform operated by progressive groups—and at no cost.

The list of technology goes on and the relevance of the platforms we used will fade quickly. We don't expect it will be helpful for readers to try and replicate exactly what we did. Instead, we wanted to demonstrate how this is a rule that social change groups can adopt to work collaboratively, cheaply, and powerfully when there are volunteers waiting to be asked to do the hard work of making change.

People New to Politics Make the Best Revolutionaries

★ zack ★

I n an exciting, growing movement, most people will probably be totally new to politics. Don't weight these enthusiastic leaders down with the old baggage of past movements. If we're not winning with the leaders we have now, why not embrace more and newer leaders?

The most pleasing thing for Becky and me about the mass volunteer meetings we held was when, in the first moments, we would ask how many people were totally new to politics. Always a majority of hands went up and sometimes up to three-quarters. What's fascinating is that this is always the case with big movements.

Each movement that brings in all these new people is a chance to build to transformational change—to take a real revolution all the way. In recent history, of course, movements have fallen far short of that. Presidential campaigns have an end date, and while there have been thoughts of keeping the revolution going—in 2004, 2008, and 2016—it hasn't happened yet. Other movements over the past few decades have also brought in tons of new people, but each of them also have eventually peaked and declined without getting to the point of real revolution that changes everything.

Each one of these campaigns or movements has left something behind that may have the same name as the movement that created it, but that is essentially a fossil of its original self. Fossils are created when the molecules of a dead creature erode away and are replaced with a different kind of molecule that forms stone. The shape of the original creature remains, but now it's stone. A similar process happens with dead movements. When it seems as if there isn't anything productive left to do, many of the most passionate and practical activists turn their focus back to all the important work they were doing in their community before the movement. In fact, they probably never stopped doing those community things during the movement.

Too often, organizations and institutions created in the movement live on past their moment in the movement. As they continue on, many passionate people who were a huge part of getting things done go back to their daily lives—and the people who are left are those who enjoy meeting and talking but not necessarily doing effective work. And this is okay because the movement died and there isn't much work to do anymore anyway!

The problem comes when a new movement starts up. Suddenly, huge numbers of new people flood in who want to work. These newbies logically look to the people who were already there, usually in what might appear to be the most relevant institutions of the left, or the progressive movement, or a political party. If the fossilized institutions leftover from past movements are allowed to play a key role in the new movement, then the new people will face all kinds of resistance as they enthusiastically try to get to work.

We've watched this happen many times over the years. It's tragic, because the new people look up to the people with roles in movement-associated institutions. They expect guidance. These new folks often have highly developed leadership qualities from their lived experience, where they are playing rich roles in their communities and forging meaningful careers that require a lot of skill. Oftentimes they are better prepared for leadership than the people they look to to set an agenda and put them to work for real change.

People who are new to politics don't bring all the baggage of the old ways things were done. Some new people bring with them so many talents and so much experience to solving problems that your campaign couldn't afford to retain them full time. And we need these people's talent and experience!

Welcoming new people is especially crucial when we're in a revolutionary or movement moment. Professionals tend to hone their skills in and tailor their plans toward fights for incremental change—they tend to practice small organizing. What works in small organizing doesn't meet the movement moment.

If people running things haven't demonstrated that they can win big meaningful change, why wouldn't we want to open up leadership to give more meaningful roles to people who aren't part of the broken system we find ourselves trapped in?

Where the greatest power lies is when there is a hybrid team of both people new to politics and professionals who are true believers, and they work side by side as peers. Our distributed organizing team on the Bernie campaign was half professionals and half super volunteers who were new to politics. It was the best team I've ever been a part of mostly because of that mix.

In every new, energetic, and growing movement we've ever participated in, the most enthusiastic and creative people have been the ones with no experience. These people often asked us for advice and asked when "the campaign" would provide the expertise they lacked. We spent a lot of our time answering that they should stop waiting for someone to bring what they lacked, because when it came to being great organizers of their community, they were far ahead of where many of the old timers and pros were.

We're thinking of people like Debra Mayes, who besides making a few calls for Obama in 2008 had never participated in politics before. Like most Bernie volunteers, Debra fit the description of a smart, hard-working American who'd done everything right and yet found herself slipping through the cracks of an economy that increasingly works for the few at the expense of the many. She lived in Los Angeles, a city that becomes more difficult for working people to survive in each year. Even though it was incredibly difficult for her economically, she traveled to other states to volunteer full time in the weeks leading up to primaries and caucuses. I met her the night of the Nevada caucus at a gathering at the house of a volunteer who, despite having a six-month-old baby, had hosted several out-of-state travelers like Debra for several weeks.

When Debra found out that I was on the national staff, she told me she wanted to talk to me privately. Saikat was there, too—and she took us both into another room and proceeded to ask us a series of questions about why the campaign had done certain things that seemed very counterproductive and not done other things that seemed obviously necessary. At first, she was hesitant and deferential, but as we kept agreeing with her about her assessments, she became bolder.

"Are we sure that all of these people are really fighting for the same thing as we are?" she said. "Or is it just a job for them?"

If the whole campaign had simply been handed over to all the new people like Debra one day, we would not have had instant utopia. The work of organizing an effective and efficient campaign operation does require experience. But one thing that could not have been more obvious to us and many others on the Bernie campaign is that to actually go all the way and win, the next revolutionary movement needs to figure out how to put the power directly into the hands of people like Debra, who are totally new to politics, because they make the best revolutionaries.

We're thinking of people like Issy Allison, who organized a team of volunteers from Charlotte, North Carolina, to spend a significant chunk of their time on the road assisting state canvassing operations in a dozen states. She and her group took ridiculous amounts of time off work, sometimes jeopardizing their jobs. Issy had worked as a trainer at a local utility company for eleven years and had never gotten involved in politics before.

We're thinking of the people who ran the Miami volunteer office for a frenetic two weeks leading up to the Florida vote. In my last weeks on the campaign as a staffer, I wound up in Florida, a state where we had a huge number of amazing volunteers, and where the campaign had decided it wasn't worth putting staff. But the campaign had rented three offices—and now wasn't sure how to open them without staff on the ground to take care of them. Paula Dorfman and I sent out an email to all the active volunteers in Miami and got a crowd of fifty people. I told them that this was their office and asked for volunteers to run it. Nearly every volunteer who stepped up was brand-new to politics.

There was Angela Barney, a young doctor still in her grueling internship, who would come to the office every day after a long shift. The first thing she would do was to pick up a mop and start cleaning the vast office.

There were Isobel Loaiza and Jenny De Sensi, who brought their small children every day and split up the shifts for staffing the door and greeting everyone who came in. And Andrea Perez, who came straight to the office every day after her marketing job to work on designs for social media and old-fashioned posters that kids were putting up all over the neighborhood to attract phone bankers. And Gregory Saint-Jean, who managed our inventory of donated laptops to drive phone banking. Nkume and Nadia Sobe, who put me up in their guest room when I was in Florida, phone-banked, and provided support to the group, even as they were hard at work building a new business.

Carlos Condarco, Erika Grohoski Peralta, Pablo Menvielle, and Zenia Perez became a crack force that ran various operations to turn out phone bankers not only to our office but also to all phone banks in the state. They used email, Text for Bernie, and social media, and after a few days of getting a system together, started filling our office to capacity every day—and it was a huge office! When Bernie surprised us with a series of Florida stadium events—Erika and Zenia introduced Bernie at the Miami event to an audience of thousands.

If I listed the names of everyone else who played a major a role in that office, it would fill a whole page.

All of this was a mad scramble in the two weeks before the primary. It was bittersweet to see it all come together, because most of us knew it was too late to matter. A huge chunk of the vote had been cast in early and mail voting.

In those two weeks, one question would come up over and over. Volunteers would say: We volunteers are running this office ourselves. We're making thousands of calls each day out of this one office. We are ready to run canvasses. We're ready to do anything. Why did the campaign wait until now to give us these resources when we could have been doing this for the past year?

I didn't have a good answer for them. But their question is clearly a statement about what needs to be different next time. Trust the people, especially the new people, with resources and know that they want nothing more than to execute a campaign's smart plan to win.

This Is How We Win

★ becky & zack ★

Revolutions are messy, wonderful, maddening, and joyful all at once. They alternate between inspiring unbelievable elation and taking your heart and crushing it in a vise, sometimes both in the same day.

Revolutions rarely succeed immediately. But when they do achieve their ultimate goal—even when it seems sudden—it's usually a result of years of accumulated confidence, new tactics, and momentum. All of this is gained through defeats and setbacks that train and galvanize an ever-growing base of people who believe that change is possible if they all stand up and fight for change together.

When Bernie called for a political revolution, his campaign was just taking its place as part of the process of bringing more people into the start of something big. Yes, we failed to win Bernie the Democratic nomination for president, even though we came excruciatingly close to doing so. But in the process, we demonstrated that a real political revolution is possible. A political revolution is something that we must grow together over the long haul. Our next step is to bring what we learned from the Bernie campaign along with all the new people that we met to the struggles you're fighting right now in your own communities, campaigns, or organizations.

Bernie began the race fairly late in the game, with 3 percent name recognition, no money, and all kinds of baggage that pundits believed would disqualify him out of hand. By the time the Iowa primary came, Bernie was surging in the national polls. He went on to win twenty-two states and received an astonishing 46 percent of the pledged delegates for the nomination.

This book is about a new set of practices and an orientation that helped make all of that possible—and we believe that it can be applied to other struggles that are part of building a political revolution to critical mass, including the one's you are fighting in right now.

On the Bernie campaign, in the later primary states where we worked, we began to unleash hundreds of thousands of volunteers to do meaningful and effective voter contact work. Even though we're excited about the results we saw, and we believe that massive volunteer voter contact efforts must have contributed in some way to Bernie's success, we know that the distributed organizing program barely scratched the surface of what Bernie's supporters were capable of achieving.

One of our greatest failures was that we were not able to win enough trust from the campaign leadership and traditional field organization for the idea of volunteer-led organizing. We failed to secure key resources and authorizations that would have allowed us to build a massive and effectively targeted campaign. That would have included rolling out VAN, the campaign voter database, to all fifty states as early as July of 2015 and giving volunteers the ability to organize their own states well before paid staff would ever land on the ground there. We also could have allowed volunteers to crowdfund and open their own offices. And we could have developed a base of volunteer leaders who then could have formed the core of paid staff when the campaign was ready to start hiring in the later states.

The problem of scaling volunteer-led field programs and integrating volunteers with traditional paid field staff is one that we are confident will be solved. First, the Bernie campaign showed us what was possible and pioneered new ways of mass organizing to make it easier for the next insurgent candidate willing to run on a big message with big organizing behind it. Second, new overtime rules issued by the Obama administration in 2016 may guarantee that it happens sooner rather than later. Paid field organizers generally put in massive amounts of hours, far in excess of the forty-hour workweek, and they do this for low wages. Under the new overtime rules, any employee making less than roughly $60,000 a year will have to be paid overtime. The traditional system we have in place will become even less scalable as the expense of paid labor will far exceed what most issue advocacy groups or political campaigns can afford (or are willing) to pay.

The Bernie campaign inspired the greatest number of volunteers ever seen in a presidential primary. We built a massive volunteer voter contact machine that made over seventy-five million phone calls, sent over eight million peer-to-peer text messages, and held more than one hundred thousand volunteer-led events. It was a start but was nowhere near the massive wave of volunteer voter contact we could have launched had we gone all-in on a grassroots approach.

There's a growing body of research that shows that television ads—the vast majority of spending in federal elections—have only a slight and fleeting impact on voters. While ads can be important in helping an unknown candidate get name recognition and thus become more viable, they have not been proven to have a substantial impact on voter turnout.

One of the things the campaign got wrong—and in some ways it's hard to blame anyone because the conventional wisdom favoring massive ad spending seems blindingly ubiquitous—was spending so much money on ads and not shifting more money into organizing. The biggest single expenditure by far of the Bernie campaign, as it is in nearly every electoral campaign at the federal or statewide level, was advertising. Bernie spent more money on advertising than any other presidential candidate in the 2016 primaries. He spent more money than Hillary Clinton, more money than the Republican candidates, and certainly more money than Donald Trump, who could count the mainstream media as a virtual SuperPAC that kept him on the air practically 24/7. Meanwhile, Clinton spent more than twice as much money on staff than our campaign did.

What the volunteers knew all along was that the gold standard in any campaign for changing hearts and minds is a personal conversation between a volunteer and a voter at the door or on the phone. We don't think of this as just as a missed opportunity—we see this as good news. The science on this continues to pile up on our side. Recent research confirms that deep, engaged conversations between volunteers and voters are not just effective in moving voters to the polls. They can change deeply held attitudes regarding controversial issues such as transgender rights, and those changed attitudes can endure over time. Person-to-person outreach can be used to turn out members to community meetings as well as to the polls, to build public support for racial justice, redistribution of wealth, climate action to achieve 100% energy independence, and other urgent causes. The nonprofit sector spends billions of dollars a year on advertising. Imagine if even just a healthy fraction of that was spent on volunteer-to-community or member-to-member outreach.

We don't know the effect that the over $90 million the campaign spent on television advertising had in states we needed to win but lost. What we do know (and what volunteers have told us repeatedly) is that in almost every state, Bernie had far more than enough volunteers mobilized early enough to build the biggest, most effective voter contact program in history. No matter what our organizing challenge—whether it's an election or a massive grassroots lobbying mission—we can change outcomes by investing early in building effective and massive person-to-person outreach campaigns. The Bernie campaign proved this was possible. Now we just need to go out and make it happen.

Imagine what would happen:

- If a huge campaign for change that tackles all the issues, with race as part of the core message to everyone, is started early enough to allow for the lead time that's required to set up an effective national grassroots organization.
- If volunteer leaders—starting at the very beginning of the campaign, not the end—are given a clear and objective way to demonstrate contributions to a centralized plan to win and are empowered by access to top-notch voter contact tools and data.
- If volunteer leaders are given the green light to run grassroots headquarters out of their homes and raise money to open public offices in their communities.
- If mass organizing barnstorms are held as weekly volunteer activation sessions in every neighborhood in every state.
- If there is a management system that allows proven volunteers to have a defined place in the organizational hierarchy, with the same oversight and accountability as staff.
- If the massive scale of the organization and the ample lead time in each state allows the campaign to rely less on

targeting and instead reach out to all the people, not just swing and base voters, but also unregistered voters, young people, and independents.

- If the campaign becomes a truly national conversation about our collective fate—a conversation held on the porch or the telephone of virtually every American.
- If tens of millions of dollars less are spent on television ads and instead those dollars are put into distributed organizing to unleash the power of the people.

So much is at stake. Every day we do not achieve radical change, we slide further toward a point of no return for our vulnerable world: wars of choice, climate change, structural racism, our out of control injustice system, poverty, addiction, the implosion of our health care system, and our inhumane immigration system. The status quo is killing people and dragging the world toward chaos.

It is with all of this on the line that we must take on the work of building and growing our political revolution. Revolutions are people's movements. People's movements are by nature big. With so many people involved and so much at stake, there's inevitably chaos. And when you go breaking all the old rules—like we're saying you should do!—it gets even more chaotic.

Bernie broke a lot of rules. He was unapologetic about the social-ist aspects of his vision for America and the world. He called for an actual political revolution. The people who answered his call—from the campaign's official staff to volunteer organizers—broke a lot of rules, too. We all saw what Bernie saw. If we kept playing by the old rules, we were going to keep getting the same results. And the status quo was literally killing people, tearing families apart, and making rampant inequality worse.

You might think that throwing out all the rules would result in anarchy. It didn't because, together with all of the volunteers, the Bernie campaign helped forge a new set of rules—rules that would help the campaign grow larger and more powerful than most of us thought possible. Rules that can now propel our movements for change to greater success faster than we would have earlier imagined.

And so even though we lost, something amazing happened. Together, we helped test, iterate, and define a new set of rules that have the power to catapult us out of the pit of incrementalism we found ourselves trapped in. We all felt the power unleashed by these new ways of doing things. That's why so many of us came out of this campaign inspired and ready to continue to take on the establishment, with all their money and their power. Because we not only know that it's possible to win, but we also learned some new ways to go about doing so.

The big vision, big goals, and big organizing that these revolutionary new rules enable, that is what this book is about. If we can put these new rules into action, and keep rewriting our rules to meet the obstacles that stand between the people and the change they want to see, then we can start to win the radical changes necessary to address the pressing issues of our time.

When you are rewriting the rules, you have to fail some of the time. That's how you learn what truly works. This is how we win.

Over the course of the Bernie campaign, we learned many things that worked better or in totally different ways than the conventional wisdom or organizing orthodoxy suggested we should do things. One of those things never failed us—volunteers who showed up with the talent, time, experience, and passion to win a big fight.

So now it's your turn. Maybe you're a volunteer who is new to activism or a professional organizer who wants to apply big organizing in your work. Take these rules. Build huge and powerful movements. Pick a lot of fights, including lots of big ones! Propose the solutions we need but the politicians say are impossible to win. Along the way you will most certainly need to improve these rules. Some of them you may need to throw out. And, of course, we look forward to seeing the new rules you write!

We want to close with a thank you from the bottom of our hearts to the leaders we worked with across hundreds of communities. There was never a discussion about who this book should be dedicated to. This book was inspired by and written for all the people who are leading in ways big and small to build the political revolution. Bernie wasn't the leader we've been waiting for. You all were.

Acknowledgments

This book is dedicated to the volunteers, but there are so many other people who played important roles in the evolution of these rules.

If you think you should have been in this book, you probably were at some point! We wrote a manuscript that was nearly twice as long as this book is now. But for all sorts of reasons—format, readability, time constraints on getting this to the printer—lots of stories and names of folks who were absolutely essential to this work couldn't make it into the final edition. So we'll make an attempt to sneak your names in here!

First and foremost we thank Senator Bernie Sanders. It was an honor to be part of his campaign. Throughout the primary, the campaign's most important asset was Bernie's message, which would never have gotten such incredible traction if it weren't for Bernie's trustworthiness and authenticity as a messenger.

We thank the distributed organizing team on the Bernie campaign, who left their jobs and joined us. A huge shout out to Claire Sandberg, our digital organizing director; Saikat Chakrabarti, who was the director of organizing technology; and "Texas" Zack Malitz, who got called up to the national team from Austin to serve as deputy digital organizing director. Sam Briggs ran the Bernie Dialer, Ceci Hall created and led so many volunteer teams, Daniel Souweine ran Text for Bernie, Jon Warnow organized the "Bernie Journey," Will Easton was in charge of organizing emails, Corbin Trent helped pioneer the barnstorm meetings and was the lynchpin of too many things to list here, Craig Grella ran the berniesanders .com help desk, and Lilia Villa was digital point on Latino outreach and so much more.

Hired from the volunteer ranks were Elijah Browning, Liam Clive, Paula Dorfman, Stephanie Nissley, Robert Reeves, Tara Reilly, and Nathan Ruby. Student organizers who started as interns but then were promoted to staff organizing positions included Max

Cotterill, Cole Edwards, Hannah Fertig, Sam Ghazey, Lynn Hua, Kyle Machado, and Alexandra Rojas. We were so lucky that the data department assigned Ari Trujillo-Wesler, who was an incredibly hard worker and cared deeply about volunteer empowerment, to the distributed organizing team. And we got to work with software developers who were deeply committed to organizing, which is rare, including Jon Culver and Jacob LeGrone.

So many super volunteers who we met and worked with on the campaign trail deeply impacted our thinking and our work—and though it would take pages to name them all, we'd like to thank Isra Allison, Aman Ardalan, Catherine Aronson, Caely Barrett, Patricia Bazemore, Karen Bernal, Scott Berry, Laksh Bhasin, Derron Black, William Blankenship, Terry Bouricius, Mario Brown, Rapi Castillo, Julie Chamberlin, Dionne Charlotte, Tania Colon, Clarice Correll, Emma Easley Darden, Jasper Davidoff, Janet Davis, Michelle Deatrick, Vrinda Deshpande, Andi Duncan, Lisa Earle, Steve Early, Kari Edwards, Christian Einfeldt, Christy Esmahan, Nicole Fairall, Michael Farar, Mike Feher, Barbara and Danny Fetonte, Rusty Fobes, Corey Frang, Teri Gidwitz, Yolanda Gonzalez, Connie Grubbs, Sibylla Guerrero, Robert Hammer, Andrew Hansen, Jen and Alun Harris, Amanda Harrity, Michael Healy, Nora Herold, Jon Hughes, Rojan Jain, Julian Janssen, Ben and Betsy Kemper, Dan Kinkler, Kelli Kuhlman, Shelley Little, Mac Lotze, Chad Lupkes, Sean McFarland, Michelle Manos, Mike Marlin, Dan Mason, Carlos Marroquin, Debra Mayes, Viviana Medina, AJ Miles, Patrick Mundy, David Nguyen, Mary Nishimuta, Lena Nitsan, Emma Optiz, Chandra Paetsch, Sarah Parrish, Alex Payne, Peachy Piana, John Raeder, Elanor Riley, Manny Rivera, Steph Rountree, Taran Samarth, Judie Schumacher, Tessa Sheehan, Josh Smith, Nkume and Nadia Sobe, Isabel Song, Alexandria Sousa, Joshue Tyler Stanley, Colleen Stanturf, Eric Sunderland, Nasim Thomson, Joe Thompson, Ryan Trundle, Atticus White, Lawrence Wilson, Haley Zink, and everyone who worked in the volunteer-led Florida field offices.

And, of course, as mentioned in the book, Bernie's digital department—including the campaign's social media, digital fundraising, website, advertising, and video media—was directed with a vision and judgment well beyond his years by Kenneth Pennington and largely led by brilliant teams within Revolution Messaging. The teams in Kenneth's department set a standard for innovation and excellence in a presidential primary that will stand for many years to come. Most notably, Hector Sigala, also from the Senate office, not only ran but dominated social media. Revolution Messaging's email fundraising crew broke record after record, led by Tim with help from Michael Whitney and Robin Curran. Tim's team raised over $231 million online in small-dollar contributions, which meant that Bernie could spend all of his time talking to voters—not flying to big-dollar donor events in the coastal capitals. Revolution Messaging's other teams on the campaign included the digital ads team led by Keegan Goudis with help from Liz Bennett, and video and creative direction led by Arun Chaudry with help from Peter O'Leary. And watching over all of Revolution Messaging's contributions was the firm's founder and Obama 2008 alumnus Scott Goodstein, who put his own punk rock stamp on so many aspects of Bernie's campaign.

There were several other more or less self-contained parts of the campaign that did amazing work with few resources under extremely difficult conditions. This isn't an exhaustive list of departments—just a rundown of a few of the best. We thank campaign leadership—Phil Fiermonte, John Robinson, and Jeff Weaver—for taking a chance on a nontraditional digital organizing program that no presidential primary campaign had ever scaled in the way that Bernie 2016 did. National field director Rich Pelletier brought the distributed organizing team under the field umbrella and supported our unorthodox approach to the work. The crack teams in Iowa and New Hampshire were led by Robert Becker and Julia Barnes. A special shout out to the amazing work of Julia Barnes, who was eventually promoted to national field director when Rich went upstairs to take the role of deputy campaign manager. Marcus Ferrell was both head of African American outreach and the southeast political director and had two of the most difficult jobs on the campaign. Our ridiculously underresourced press team was held together from the beginning by a young staffer who had never worked on a campaign before—Arianna Jones.

Michael Briggs, from Bernie's Senate office, did an astonishing job with only half his time allocated to the campaign; and Mike Casca, also from the Senate side, was genius at rapid response.

Nick Carter, one of the campaign's very first hires and one of the absolute nicest people working in the Burlington headquarters, was the lone political staffer tasked with racking up endorsements for Bernie and so much more. Our advance team, led by Mark Levitt, who had worked in advance with Obama 2012 and with the White House, was terrifyingly effective and efficient. Everyone knows how great our stadium rallies were. What they don't know is that Mark's team pulled those events together in sometimes only seventy-two—or even fewer—hours. Mark's team pulled off miracles and also handled travel for the entire staff. Matt Berg was a superhero who did at least four jobs on our campaign, each of which is a whole department on a traditional presidential campaign. Luis Calderin, our art, culture, and youth vote director, made a lot of unimaginable things happen, including magic moments like Bernie's interview with Killer Mike.

The People for Bernie, an independent social media effort led by Winnie Wong and Charles Lenchner, deserves its own book, which we hope they are writing. Millennials for Bernie Sanders, now Millennials for Revolution, gives us such hope, and we thank Moumita Ahmed particularly for her leadership. The nurses got their own rule, but we have to name some names here. There couldn't be better people to follow into battle than the National Nurses United's chief RoseAnn DeMoro and her team, including Michael Lighty, Bonnie Castillo, and Holly Miller. A special shout out to California Nurses Association volunteers Carolyn Bowden and Anne Olivia Eldred.

Solidarity Strategies, led by Chuck Rocha wasn't the campaign's Latino consulting group, they were consultants on the national voter contact program who happened to be Latino. Solidarity printed nearly fifteen million pieces of literature for the campaign and played a key role in recruiting and hiring staff. No doubt, Chuck helped build an outstanding Latino outreach team started by Arturo Carmona and later led by Bill Velasquez. That department—and especially the young Dreamers Cesar Vargas and Erika Andiola—tirelessly educated, activated, and mobilized the Latino community.

Democracy for America was one of our closest outside partners in the work we did on the distributed organizing team. Executive Director Charles Chamberlain allowed Annie Weinberg, DFA's electoral director, to take unpaid time off to join the campaign at a critical moment, and his organization helped the campaign by recruiting volunteers and raising money directly into our campaign coffers. They were model allies.

We want to thank all the organizations, elected officials, and candidates for office who endorsed Bernie and helped raise money and recruit volunteers for the campaign. We'd especially like to recognize among elected officials and candidates Rep. Raul Grijalva, Rep. Keith Ellison, Rep. Tulsi Gabbard, Rep. Rick Nolan, Sen. Jeff Merkley, former Ohio State Senator Nina Turner, former Nevada State Assemblymember Lucy Flores, Washington State Senator Pramila Jayapal, and Zephyr Teachout. We'd especially like to recognize among endorsing organizations Communication Workers of America, MoveOn.org, United Electrical Workers, American Postal Workers Union, Amalgamated Transit Union, Democracy for America, National Nurses United, California Nurses Association, National People's Action, Working Families Party, Progressive Democrats of America, Friends of the Earth, Climate Hawks Vote, and the International Longshore and Warehouse Union.

We'd like thank the groups fighting fascism and austerity around the world whom Ben Brandzel and Becky Jarvis invited us to address as an important early audience for these concepts. These groups include New Zealand's ActionStation, Poland's Akcja Demokracja, South Africa's Amandla, Austria's Aufstehn, Romania's de-clic, India's Jhatkaa, Italy's Progressi, Sweden's Skiftet (whose staff helped spearhead "Sweden for Bernie"), Ireland's Uplift, and Israel's Zazim. We are in awe of how they are addressing struggles in their own countries with courage, ingenuity, and inspiration.

Zack Malitz read the entire manuscript while flying between battleground states on airplanes and offered valuable additions, subtractions, and corrections. Saikat Chakrabarti, Elijah Zarlin, and James Rucker read the early drafts of some of these rules and provided super helpful feedback.

Many thanks to the Wallace Global Fund for providing the resources to enable us to take what we've learned out to social change organizers in the United States and around the world. Steve Lyons helped us design an open source presentation we hope will help former Bernie staffers and volunteers alike share and teach these rules.

Allison Barlow provided sharp perspective and kind encouragement, without which this book might never have been written. Annie Leonard met with us early in the project, offering equal parts encouragement and wisdom. Libby Lenkinski provided helpful feedback and encouragement. Steve Cobble offered wisdom and inspiration from insurgent campaigns of past presidential cycles. Rashad Robinson and Arisha Hatch at ColorOfChange have inspired us with their pioneering efforts to scale peer-to-peer text messaging in the fight for black liberation, and we look forward to learning from their work. Judith Freeman, who worked on Obama 2008 and cofounded the New Organizing Institute, was generous with her wise perspective and actionable advice. We received questions and support during a brief and welcome break from writing when Saikat Chakrabarti, Matt DeBergalis, Jin Ding, Arisha Hatch, Heidi Hess, Michael Kieschnick, Michael Lighty, Zack Malitz, Sheena Pakanati, Ben Rahn, James Rucker, Daniel Souweine, and Elijah Zarlin visited us while we were on retreat.

We're both grateful to the staff of CREDO Action—Jin Ding, Heidi Hess, Jordan Krueger, Josh Nelson, Shant Mesrobian, Carrie Olson, Mark Ristaino, Murshed Zaheed, and Elijah Zarlin—who were so amazing that Becky was able to confidently hand over the reins and devote herself 24/7 to the Bernie campaign. And to the staff and volunteers of Brand New Congress, many of whom appear in the pages of this book, who let Zack disappear for six weeks to collaborate on the manuscript.

Becky would like to thank Michael Kieschnick, Sandy Newman, Myles Taylor, Harriet Barlow, Heather Booth, Mark Ritchie, Matt Stoller, Donald Green, David Broockman, and Josh Kalla for teaching her so much about why elections matter and how to win them.

Zack would like to thank all the union members and unorganized workers who pulled his head out of his ass and taught him how to organize; Joan Blades, Wes Boyd, Carrie Olson, and Eli Pariser for showing him how to operate on a national stage and how great a healthy, productive work environment could be; and Frank O'Brien and so many at ThoughtWorks for giving him a place to call home (and a paycheck) so that he didn't need to ever call it quits.

We have to thank Margo Baldwin for so many things but perhaps first and foremost for her revolutionary posts on Facebook throughout the primary campaign. This was how we knew that she would be the perfect partner for publishing this book. When we approached her about our idea for a book back in June, she was generous with her time and advice. Once we got started, she coached us through the entire process, offering positive reinforcement along with the directive feedback we desperately needed. Had Margo not told us, via a Skype call to a small conference room where we were camped out in a Berlin hotel, that our sample chapters and outline were all wrong, we never would have gotten this book to press. Once we were headed in the right direction with our drafts, she brought in the full force of Chelsea Green's resources along with the amazing Brianne Goodspeed to be our editor. The draft we delivered to Chelsea Green was on time but about twice as long as it needed to be. We literally don't know how Brianne plucked this book out of the chaos we submitted and can't thank her enough for her efforts. Working as a team with a publisher that shared our commitment to people-powered revolution was truly a gift. We couldn't be more grateful that Margo and Brianne brought together such a great team at Chelsea Green to help turn our manuscript into a book and get it out into the world, including Kate Adams, Angela Boyle, Alex Bullett, Christina Butt, Joan Cushman, Sandi Eaton, Makenna Goodman, Tim Halteman, Chris Hopkins, Melissa Jacobson, Darrell Koerner, Sean Maher, Fern Marshall Bradley, Michael Metivier, Joni Praded, Jenna Stewart, Patricia Stone, Shay Totten, Ben Watson, Michael Weaver, and Kirsten Wilson.

Finally, we want to thank the people who are the most dear to us in the world.

Becky thanks Emily, the love of her life. She didn't hesitate to say yes when Becky floated the idea of giving up her salary and steady job to go out on the road (and be constantly away, preoccupied, stressed out, and absent for every important holiday, birthday, and anniversary for months) to help build the revolution. Literally nothing would be possible for Becky without Emily's love and her shared and deep commitment to social change.

Zack above all thanks his wife, Elizabeth, and daughter, Esther, who was six years old during the Bernie campaign. They were heroically supportive as he spent more than half his time on the road, took a big pay cut, and dragged them to Burlington for a couple of months. Zack is eternally grateful for the sacrifice, trust, and love that made his time with the Bernie campaign possible.

Timeline

APRIL 16, 2015: Bernie Sanders walks out of the Senate and announces he is running for the Democratic nomination for the presidency. The People for Bernie launches with an open letter.

JULY 6: Zack Exley flies to Washington, DC, and starts work on the campaign as a senior advisor, planning a massive wave of volunteer campaign kick-off events announced for July 29th. A week later Claire Sandberg joins the team as the digital organizing director.

JULY 13: Zack sets up the first volunteer team, the berniesanders .com Help Desk.

JULY 17: A Black Lives Matter protest disrupts the Democratic candidate forum at the Netroots Nation conference.

JULY 29: 100,000 supporters attend 2,700 house parties and watch Bernie Sanders livestream. Over 45,000 people sign up to volunteer for the campaign.

AUGUST 4: Zack moves to Burlington, Vermont, and, over a series of phone calls, recruits Corbin Trent to join the campaign.

LATE AUGUST: Becky Bond tells Zack that, if he can get her hired onto his team, she'll leave her job and join the campaign.

SEPTEMBER 11: Saikat Chakrabarti joins the campaign as director of organizing technology.

SEPTEMBER 23: Becky interviews in Burlington.

OCTOBER 1: Fundraising numbers come out and, astonishingly, Bernie is outpacing Barack Obama's 2008 campaign fundraising.

OCTOBER 2: Becky gets a job on the campaign as a senior advisor.

OCTOBER 13: The first Democratic primary debate is held, with over 4,000 Bernie Sanders debate watch parties launched by the distributed organizing team.

OCTOBER 20: Zack and Corbin pilot an early version of barnstorm meetings in Tennessee.

OCTOBER 28: The national student town hall livestream is held with Bernie Sanders and members of College Students for Bernie Sanders.

NOVEMBER: Zack and Becky barnstorm across Colorado and meet volunteers who are already canvassing for the March 1, 2016, caucus without access to the VAN.

NOVEMBER 14: The second Democratic primary debate is held; attendees at thousands of debate watch parties are asked to launch phone banks.

DECEMBER 12–16: The distributed organizing team meets for the first time in person in Seattle.

DECEMBER 13: A barnstorm in Seattle creates 80 phone banks that the team is unable to fill with RSVPs.

DECEMBER 15: The Bernie Dialer is launched in Oakland, California, with volunteers from National Nurses United.

DECEMBER 19: The third Democratic primary debate is held.

LATE DECEMBER: The distributed organizing team is granted 10 hires by the new national field director, Rich Pelletier.

MID JANUARY, 2016: Orange County Community College interns are hired and drive across the country to Burlington.

JANUARY 17: The fourth Democratic primary debate is held.

JANUARY 21: Becky and "Texas" Zack Malitz train volunteers to run barnstorms in a Texas pilot program.

FEBRUARY 1: Bernie fights to a virtual tie in the Iowa Caucus, though Clinton captures a slight delegate lead.

EARLY FEBRUARY: Daniel Souweine and Sam Ghazey launch Text for Bernie.

FEBRUARY 9: Bernie wins the New Hampshire primary by the greatest margin in history.

FEBRUARY 23: Bernie loses the Nevada caucuses. Zack Malitz moves up to the national distributed organizing team from the Texas state team.

FEBRUARY 26: Zack Exley heads to Miami to open volunteer-run field offices in advance of the March 15 primary.

FEBRUARY 27: Bernie loses the South Carolina primary by a wide margin.

MARCH 1: Super Tuesday primaries and caucuses are held in: Alabama (loss), Arkansas (loss), Colorado (win), Georgia (loss), Massachusetts (loss by just 1.5 points), Minnesota (win), Oklahoma (win), Tennessee (loss), Texas (loss), Vermont (win), and Virginia (loss).

MARCH 5: Kansas (win), Louisiana (loss), and Nebraska (win) vote.

MARCH 6: Maine (win) caucus is held.

MARCH 8: Michigan (surprise win) and Mississippi (loss) vote.

MARCH 15: Florida (loss), Illinois (loss), Missouri (virtual tie—lost by less than 2,000 votes), North Carolina (loss), and Ohio (loss) vote.

MARCH 16: Zack Exley leaves the Bernie campaign and starts working with super volunteers to found Brand New Congress.

MARCH 22: Arizona (loss), Idaho (win), and Utah (win) vote.

MARCH 26: Alaska (win), Hawaii (win), and Washington (win) vote.

APRIL 5: Wisconsin (win) votes.

APRIL 9: Wyoming (win) votes.

APRIL 16: New York (loss) votes.

APRIL 26: Connecticut (loss), Delaware (loss), Maryland (loss), Pennsylvania (loss), and Rhode Island (win) vote.

APRIL 27: There is a mass layoff at the Bernie campaign. Becky is laid off from the campaign along with 75 percent of distributed organizing team.

MAY 3: Indiana (win) votes.

MAY 10: West Virginia (win) votes.

MAY 17: Kentucky (loss by less than 2 points) and Oregon (win) vote.

JUNE 7: California (loss), Montana (win), New Jersey (loss), New Mexico (loss), North Dakota (win), and South Dakota (loss by less than 1,200 votes) vote.

JUNE 14: Washington, DC, (loss) votes.

JULY 25: The Democratic National Committee convention is held.

About the Authors

Photo by Bloomberg / Getty Images

BECKY BOND served as a senior advisor on the Bernie Sanders presidential campaign and was an architect of the campaign's national, volunteer-driven grassroots campaign. Prior to joining the Bernie Sanders campaign, Becky served as political director at CREDO where she was an innovator working at the intersection of organizing, politics, and technology for over a decade. Becky is a cofounder of CREDO SuperPAC, which was named by *Mother Jones* as one "2012's Least Horrible Super-PACs" for helping to defeat five sitting Tea Party Republican Congressmen. She lives in San Francisco, California, with writer, designer, and book artist Emily McVarish.

ZACK EXLEY served as a senior advisor on the Bernie Sanders presidential campaign and was an architect of the campaign's national, volunteer-driven grassroots campaign. Zack was a union organizer before becoming MoveOn.org's first organizing director in its campaign to prevent the war in Iraq in 2003. As an early advisor to the Howard Dean campaign, he helped transfer MoveOn.org's early fundraising and organizing discoveries into presidential politics, and he then served as John Kerry's director of online fundraising and communications in the general election where his team raised more than $100 million online for the nominee. Subsequently, Zack worked as a consultant to global NGOs, campaigns, and companies, and served as Wikipedia's chief community officer and chief revenue officer. He lives in the Ozarks with his wife, Elizabeth, and daughter, Esther.

For more information about Becky, Zack, *Rules for Revolutionaries*, and a downloadable, open-source teaching tool to help you implement change in your community, visit www.bigorganizing.com.

green
press
INITIATIVE

Chelsea Green Publishing is committed to preserving ancient forests and natural resources. We elected to print this title on paper containing 100% postconsumer recycled paper, processed chlorine-free. As a result, for this printing, we have saved:

172 Trees (40' tall and 6-8" diameter)
80,208 Gallons of Wastewater
77 million BTUs Total Energy
5,369 Pounds of Solid Waste
14,789 Pounds of Greenhouse Gases

Chelsea Green Publishing made this paper choice because we are a member of the Green Press Initiative, a nonprofit program dedicated to supporting authors, publishers, and suppliers in their efforts to reduce their use of fiber obtained from endangered forests. For more information, visit www.greenpressinitiative.org.

Environmental impact estimates were made using the Environmental Defense Paper Calculator. For more information visit: www.papercalculator.org.

the politics and practice of sustainable living

CHELSEA GREEN PUBLISHING

Chelsea Green Publishing sees books as tools for effecting cultural change
and seeks to empower citizens to participate in reclaiming our global commons and
become its impassioned stewards. If you enjoyed reading *Rules for Revolutionaries*,
please consider these other great books related to progressive politics.

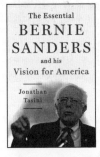

THE ALL NEW DON'T THINK OF AN ELEPHANT!
Know Your Values and Frame the Debate
GEORGE LAKOFF
9781603585941
Paperback • $15.00

THE ESSENTIAL BERNIE SANDERS
AND HIS VISION FOR AMERICA
JONATHAN TASINI
9781603586672
Paperback • $14.00

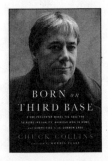

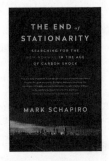

BORN ON THIRD BASE
*A One Percenter Makes the Case
for Tackling Inequality, Bringing Wealth Home,
and Committing to the Common Good*
CHUCK COLLINS
9781603586832
Paperback • $17.95

THE END OF STATIONARITY
*Searching for the New Normal
in the Age of Carbon Shock*
MARK SCHAPIRO
9781603586801
Paperback • $17.95

the politics and practice of sustainable living

For more information or to request a catalog,
visit **www.chelseagreen.com** or
call toll-free **(800) 639-4099**.